The Many Causes, of Unbelief

Bert Thompson, Ph.D.

APOLOGETICS PRESS

Apologetics Press, Inc.
230 Landmark Drive
Montgomery, Alabama 36117-2752

TABLE OF CONTENTS

DEDICATION

This volume is dedicated to the elders [Don Brannan, Bill Couch, Howard Jones, J.T. Norton, and Ted Norton] of the Eastern Meadows Church of Christ in Montgomery, Alabama whose moral and financial support of the author's efforts, and of the work of Apologetics Press, have been both unwavering and deeply appreciated.

1
INTRODUCTION

One of the most mind-numbing mysteries for those who believe in God is trying to understand the unbelief of those who do not. As one who writes and lectures often on the topics of apologetics and evidences, I frequently am asked, "What causes people **not** to believe in God?" Generally speaking, the motive behind the question is not derogatory, but complimentary. That is to say, the querist really is asking: "Why is it that **obviously intelligent** people do not believe in God?"

Neither inquiry is easy to answer because usually the person asking the question wants a simple, quick, concise response. It is difficult for the querist to understand why people who are "obviously intelligent" refuse to believe in God. It has been my experience that rarely is there a single reason for unbelief, because rarely is there a single reason that can explain adequately why a person thinks, or acts, as he does.

Surely, however, a part of the answer has to do with the fact that when God created humans, He endowed us with **freedom of choice** (often referred to as "personal volition" or "free moral agency"). This stands to reason, considering Who God is. The Bible describes Him as being, among other things, a God of love (1

John 4:8). Even a cursory survey of the Scriptures documents God's desire that man, as the zenith of His creation, possess, and employ, the freedom of choice with which he has been endowed. The truth of the matter is that God did not create mankind as some kind of robot to serve Him slavishly without any personal choice in the matter.

For example, when Joshua—who had led the Israelite nation so faithfully for so long—realized that his days were numbered and his hours were few, he assembled the entirety of that nation before him and, in one of the most moving, impassioned pleas recorded within the pages of Holy Writ, admonished his charges to employ their personal volition in a proper fashion.

> And if it seem evil unto you to serve Jehovah, choose you this day whom ye will serve; whether gods which your fathers served that were beyond the River, or the gods of the Amorites, in whose land ye dwell: but as for me and my house, we will serve Jehovah (Joshua 24:15).

Joshua's point could not have been any clearer. The Israelites, individually and collectively, had the ability, and yes, even the God-given right, to choose whether they wished to follow Jehovah. As the text continues, it indicates that on this particular occasion they chose correctly.

> And the people answered and said, Far be it from us that we should forsake Jehovah, to serve other gods.... And Israel served Jehovah all the days of Joshua, and all the days of the elders that outlived Joshua, and had known all the work of Jehovah that he had wrought for Israel (Joshua 24:16,31).

Years later, however, the people of Israel—employing that same heaven-sent personal volition—freely chose to abandon their belief in, and obedience to, God. Judges 2:10-11 records:

> [T]here arose another generation after them, that knew not Jehovah, nor yet the work which he had wrought for Israel. And the children of Israel did that which was evil in the sight of Jehovah, and served the Baalim.

Within the pages of the New Testament, the principle is the same. When Jesus condemned the self-righteousness of the Pharisees in John 5:39-40, He made this observation: "Ye search the scriptures, because ye think that in them ye have eternal life; and these are they which bear witness of me; and ye **will not** come to me, that ye may have life." The Pharisees of New Testament times possessed the same freedom of choice as the Israelites of Old Testament times. But while the Israelites to whom Joshua spoke chose at first to heed his plea and obey Jehovah, the Pharisees to whom Christ spoke chose to ignore His plea and to disobey God.

Two chapters later, when Jesus addressed the Jews in their own temple, the text indicates that they marveled at His teaching (John 7:15). But Jesus demurred, and said: "My teaching is not mine, but his that sent me. If any man **willeth** to do his will, he shall know of the teaching, whether it is of God, or whether I speak from myself" (John 7:16-17). Jesus' point to the devout temple Jews was no different than the one He had made earlier to the legalistic Pharisees. God has imbued mankind with the ability to **choose**. If a person **wills**, he can accept God and His teaching, but God never will force Himself on that person. As the apostle John brought the book of Revelation to a close, he wrote: "He that will, let him take the water of life freely" (Revelation 22:17). The operative phrase here, of course, is "he that will."

But what of he that **will not**? Freedom is accompanied by responsibility. With freedom of choice comes the responsibility to think carefully, choose wisely, and act forcefully. Freedom of choice always works best when tempered with wisdom and good judgment. Thus, in every human activity the process of recognizing, believing, and properly utilizing truth is vitally important. Especially is this true in the spiritual realm. Jesus tried to impress this upon His generation when He said: "Ye shall know the truth, and the truth shall make you free" (John 8:32). What we as humans so often fail to realize is that we are not involved in a search for truth because **it** is lost; we are involved in a search for truth because without it **we** are!

Some, however, have elected to employ their freedom of choice to ignore the truth regarding God's existence and to disobey His Word. They are the spiritual descendants of the first-century Pharisees; they **could** come to a knowledge of the truth, but they **will not**. The simple fact of the matter is that we are responsible for what we choose to believe. Using the personal volition with which God has endowed us, we may choose freely to believe in Him, or we may choose just as freely to disbelieve. The choice is up to each individual. And once that individual has made up his mind to disbelieve, God will not deter him, as Paul made clear when he wrote his second epistle to the Thessalonians. In that letter, he spoke first of those who "received not the love of the truth" (2:10), and then went on to say that "for this cause God sendeth them a working of error, that they should believe a lie" (2 Thessalonians 2:11).

What, exactly, was Paul suggesting? Was the apostle teaching that God **purposely** causes men to believe error? No, he was not. Paul's point in this passage was that we may choose to accept something as the truth when, in fact, it is false. Because God has granted man personal volition, and because He has provided within the Bible the rules, regulations, and guidelines to govern that personal volition, He therefore will refrain from overriding man's freedom of choice—even when that choice violates His law. God will not contravene man's decisions, or interfere with the actions based on those decisions. The prophet Isaiah recorded God's words on this subject many years before when he wrote:

> Yea, they have chosen their own ways, and their soul delighteth in their abominations: I also will choose their delusions, and will bring their fears upon them; because when I called, none did answer; when I spake, they did not hear: but they did that which was evil in mine eyes, and chose that wherein I delighted not (Isaiah 66:3-4).

Concerning the people who refused to have God in their knowledge, and who exchanged truth for error, Paul repeatedly stated that "God gave them up" (Romans 1:24,26,28). In his commentary on the Thessalonian epistles, Raymond C. Kelcy addressed the fact that men often prefer the consequences of a certain belief system, and that as a result

> God gives the man over to the belief of the lie which he prefers. In a sense it might be said that the means by which a person is deceived is God's permissive agency—not God's direct agency (1968, p. 157).

There is an exact parallel in the instance of the Pharaoh who sparred with Moses and Aaron over the release of the Hebrews from Egyptian bondage. When these two brothers arrived at Pharaoh's court as God's ambassadors to demand the release of the enslaved Israelites, they told the pagan potentate: "Thus saith Jehovah, the God of Israel, 'Let my people go'." Pharaoh's response, preserved in Scripture for posterity, foreshadowed the attitude of millions of unbelievers who would imitate the militant monarch's demeanor of disbelief throughout the course of human history: "Who is Jehovah, that I should hearken unto his voice to let Israel go? **I know not Jehovah**, and moreover I will not let Israel go" (Exodus 5:1-2, emp. added).

Several times the biblical text records that it was God Who "hardened Pharaoh's heart" (Exodus 7:3; 9:12; 10:1, 20,27; 11:10; 14:8). Are we to understand, therefore, that God **caused** Pharaoh's stubborn attitude of disbelief? Certainly not. The simple fact of the matter is that God did not cause Pharaoh to harden his heart and disobey, but instead **permitted** the ruler's actions. The Scriptures speak to this point when they acknowledge that Pharaoh himself "hardened his heart" (Exodus 8:15,32; 9:34-35). In their commentary on the Pentateuch, Keil and Delitzsch addressed Pharaoh's hardness of heart, even after he witnessed the miraculous plagues sent by God.

> After every one of these miracles, it is stated that Pharaoh's heart was firm, or dull, i.e. insensible to the voice of God, and unaffected by the miracles performed before his eyes, and the judgments of God suspended over him and his king-

dom.... Thus Pharaoh would not bend his self-will to the will of God, even after he had discerned the finger of God and the omnipotence of Jehovah in the plagues suspended over him and his nation; he would not withdraw his haughty refusal, notwithstanding the fact that he was obliged to acknowledge that it was sin against Jehovah. Looked at from this side, the hardening was a fruit of sin, a consequence of that self-will, high-mindedness, and pride which flow from sin, and a continuous and ever increasing **abuse of that freedom of the will** which is innate in man, and which involves the possibility of obstinate resistance to the word and chastisement of God even until death (1981, pp. 454,455, emp. added).

Pharaoh's hard heart was not God's doing, but his own. God's **permissive agency** was involved, but not His **direct agency.** That is to say, He allowed Pharaoh to use (or abuse, as Keil and Delitzsch correctly noted) his freedom of will in a vain attempt to thwart God's plans. Throughout history, God's actions have been consistent in this regard. The psalmist wrote:

> But my people hearkened not to my voice; and Israel would not hear me. So I let them go after the stubbornness of their heart, that they might walk in their own counsels (81:11-12).

Concerning the rebellious Israelites, Paul wrote in Romans 11:8 (quoting from Isaiah 29:10): "God gave them a spirit of stupor, eyes that they should not see, and ears that they should not hear." In every generation, God has granted mankind the freedom of self-determination to be blind to His existence, and in so doing to believe a lie. E.M. Zerr put it well when he said:

> The Bible in no place teaches that God ever forces a man to sin, then punishes him for the wrong-doing. Neither does He compel man against his will to do right, but has always offered him proper inducements for righteous conduct, then left it to his own responsibility to decide what he will do about it (1952, 5:159).

The same principles operate even today, almost two thousand years later. If an acknowledgment of God's existence and obedience to His Word make us free (John 8:32), surely, then, disbelief and disobedience make us captives of one sort or another. Set adrift in a vast sea of confusing and contradictory world views, we then find ourselves susceptible to every ill-conceived plan, deceptive scheme, and false concept that the winds of change may blow our way.

We become captives to error because we have abandoned the one moral compass—the existence of God—that possesses the ability to show us the way, and thereby to set us free.

2
THE MANY FACES OF UNBELIEF

Throughout history, unbelief has worn many masks. But behind each is a Pharaoh-like spirit of rebellion that—in angry defiance—raises a clenched fist to God in a display of unrepentant determination **not** to believe in Him. An examination of the many faces, and causes, of unbelief is both informative and instructive.

Atheism

In his book, *If There's a God, Why Are There Atheists?*, R.C. Sproul noted in regard to theism that "literally, the word means 'Godism,' that is belief in God. It is derived from *theos*, the Greek word for God" (1978, p. 16). Chief among unbelievers, then, would be the **atheist** (*a*, without; *theos*, God)—the person who affirms that there is no God. As Sproul went on to observe: "Atheism involves the rejection of any form of theism. To be an atheist is to disavow belief in any kind of god or gods" (p. 18). In his thought-provoking book, *Intellectuals Don't Need God*, Alister McGrath noted:

The atheist is prepared to concede—no, that is too negative a word, to **celebrate**—the need for commitment and
the existence of evidence to move one in the direction of
that commitment. In other words, the atheist recognizes
the need to come off the fence and the fact that there are
factors in the world of human experience and thought that
suggest which side of the fence that ought to be. At present, the atheist happens to sit on the godless side of that
fence (1993, p. 81, emp. in orig.).

Bruce Lockerbie, in *Dismissing God*, referred to atheism as
"the abdication of belief," and described the person who falls into this category.

For the ardent disbeliever, the hypothesis and its given
propositions are one and the same: **God does not exist**.... All that has energized the human imagination and mo-
tivated the human spirit with prospects of nirvana, the Ely-
sian Fields, the happy hunting grounds, paradise, or heav-
en—all that is meant when the Book of Ecclesiastes declares
that God "has set eternity in the hearts of men"—must be in-
validated by counterclaims of atheism (1998, pp. 225,
227, emp. in orig.).

This, no doubt, explains why a famous unbeliever like the late
Carl Sagan, the eminent atheist/astronomer of Cornell University,
opened his television extravaganza *Cosmos* (and his book by the
same name) with these words: "The Cosmos is all that is or ever
was or ever will be" (1980, p. 4). Commenting on the exclusivity
of that statement, D. James Kennedy wrote: "That is as clear a
statement of atheism as one could ever hear" (1997, p. 61).

Declaring oneself to be an atheist, however, is much easier than
defending the concept of atheism. Think of it this way. In order
to defend atheism, a person would have to know **every single
fact** there is to know, because the one fact that avoided detec-
tion might just be the fact of the existence of God. Theodore
Christlieb noted:

The denial of the existence of God involves a perfectly
monstrous hypothesis; it is, when looked at more closely,
an unconscionable assumption. Before one can say that

the world is without a God, he must first have become thoroughly conversant with the whole world.... In short, to be able to affirm authoritatively that no God exists, a man must be omniscient and omnipresent, that is, he himself must be God, and then after all there would be one (1878, pp. 143,144).

Impossible task, that—since one would have to **be** God in order to state with certainty that there is no God! Yet, as apologist Dan Story has pointed out,

...[T]his fact stops few atheists from arguing against the existence of God. Rather than admitting (or even recognizing) the irrationality of their own position, many atheists attempt to remove the rationality of the Christian position.... These atheists argue that because they don't believe in God, because their belief is negative, they don't have to martial any arguments in their favor (1997, p. 20).

Evidence of such a stance abounds. Atheistic writer George H. Smith, in his book, *Atheism: The Case Against God*, wrote:

Proof is applicable only in the case of a positive belief. To demand proof of the atheist, the religionist must represent atheism as a positive belief requiring substantiation. When the atheist is seen as a person who lacks belief in a god, it becomes clear that he is not obligated to "prove" anything. The atheist *qua* atheist does not believe anything requiring demonstration; the designation of "atheist" tells us, not what he believes to be true, but what he does **not** believe to be true. If others wish for him to accept the existence of a god, it is their responsibility to argue for the truth of theism—but the atheist is not similarly required to argue for the truth of atheism (1979, p. 16, emp. in orig.)

Such a view, however, is seriously flawed for at least two reasons. First, theists do not make the statement, "God exists," with wild abandon, expecting it to be accepted as if somehow it were spoken by divine fiat. Rather, when they defend God's existence, theists offer **evidence** to back up their case (e.g., the cosmological argument, teleological argument, moral argument, etc.)—which places the matter of the existence of God in an entirely different perspective. As Story properly noted:

> Christians have given ample evidence for the existence of the Judeo-Christian God. In light of this, if atheists claim God does not exist, they must be prepared to explain why. When Christians state that God exists and offer evidences to support this claim, they have moved the debate into a new arena—an arena in which atheists must prove that the Christian **evidences** are erroneous (1997, p. 20, emp. in orig.).

If **evidence** for God's existence has been set forth, the atheist has a responsibility (if he expects his world view to be considered seriously and accepted intellectually) to show **why** such evidence is not legitimate. After all, the Law of Rationality (one of the foundational laws of human thought) states that one should draw only those conclusions for which there is adequate and justifiable evidence. Indifference to such evidence—in light of the claim made by the atheist that God does not exist—could prove to be suicidal philosophically. The evidence just might document the theist's claim. And in the process, the atheist just might be proven wrong!

Second, in his book, *Dismissing God*, under the chapter heading, "When Disbelief Has Gone," Bruce Lockerbie rightly remarked:

> To **disbelieve** necessitates the possibility of a reasonable alternative, namely to **believe**. So "when disbelief has gone" means that the secular mind has passed even beyond this stage of contesting with Christian orthodoxy, no longer deigning to concern itself with the fantasies of faith (1998, p. 228, emp. in orig.).

While it may be the case that the modern-day unbeliever no longer deigns to concern himself with what he views as "fantasies of faith," such an attitude does nothing to address the evidence presented by the theist. Nor does indifference to the theist's evidence on the part of the atheist do anything to establish whatever type of unbelief the atheist wishes to recommend in its place. Lockerbie is correct: "To **disbelieve** necessitates the possibility of a reasonable alternative, namely to **believe**." Thus, the atheist shoulders two burdens: (1) to prove the theist's evidence is invalid; and (2) to establish—with attending evidence—a belief system that is a "reasonable alternative" worthy of acceptance by rational, thinking people.

Neither of these tasks is simple (or, theists would suggest, possible). One problem that, by necessity, would have to be broached from the outset is this. For whatever reason(s), many atheists appear unwilling to consider the evidence in the first place. Robert Gorham Davis is a retired professor of English at Harvard University who spends much of his time writing letters to the editor of the *New York Times* in order to take exception to any published reference to religion in that newspaper. In one such letter to the editor, he wrote:

> On no clear evidence theologians and philosophers declare God to be omniscient and omnicompetent. Plainly **if there were such a God who really wished to reveal Himself to mankind, He could do so in a way that left no doubt** (1992, emp. added).

That God **did** reveal Himself "in a way that left no doubt" is made clear from such evidence as: (1) the marvelous order and complexity of the macrocosm we call the Universe; (2) the intricate, delicately balanced nature of life; (3) the deliberate design inherent in the microcosm we know as the incomparable genetic code; (4) the astounding historical testimony attesting to the miracle-working Son of God; and (5) an otherwise unexplained (and unexplainable) empty tomb on a Sunday morning almost two thousand years ago. Each of these pieces of evidence (plus many more like them) helps form the warp and woof of the fabric whose purpose it is to document God's eternal existence.

That the atheist does not consider the evidence to be trustworthy or adequate to the task **does not negate the evidence**. A man's attitude toward the truth does not alter the truth. As Winfried Corduan stated in his book, *Reasonable Faith*:

> An argument, in order to be considered sound, must have true premises and valid logic. Because we think within the context of world views, someone may not be convinced by a perfectly sound argument. This is an everyday occurrence in all human reasoning and attempts at persuasion. **That is no fault of the argument**... (1993, p. 106, emp. added).

A good example of this point would be the late evolutionist and atheist, Isaac Asimov, who once admitted quite bluntly: "Emotionally, I am an atheist. I don't have the evidence to prove that God doesn't exist, but I so strongly suspect he doesn't that I don't want to waste my time" (1982, p. 9). Such a boast is easy enough to understand and requires no additional explanation. Yes, Dr. Asimov was indeed a committed atheist. However, he did not hold this view because he was able to offer adequate, legitimate reasons to justify his unbelief. Rather, his world view was an emotional response that resulted from his personal freedom of choice. The fact remains that after everything is said and done, the atheist's first option—disproving the theist's evidence—is a difficult challenge that many choose not to accept.

What, then, about option number two—providing, with attending evidence, a belief system that is a "reasonable alternative"? That, too, apparently is beyond the pale of atheism. In 1989, Richard Dawkins, renowned atheist and evolutionist of Oxford University, authored a book by the title of *The Selfish Gene* in which he discussed at great length the gene's role in the naturalistic process of "survival of the fittest." Dawkins admitted that, according to the evolutionary paradigm, genes are "selfish" because they will do whatever it takes to ensure that the individual in which they are stored produces additional copies of the genes. In commenting on the effects of such a concept on society as a whole, Dr. Dawkins lamented: "My own feeling is that a human society based simply on the gene's law of universal ruthlessness **would be a very nasty society in which to live**" (1989b, p. 3, emp. added).

Michael Ruse, a Canadian philosopher, and Edward O. Wilson, a Harvard entomologist, had made the same point four years earlier when they wrote under the title of "Evolution and Ethics":

> Morality, or more strictly **our belief in morality, is merely an adaptation put in place to further our reproductive ends**.... Ethics is seen to have a solid foundation, not in divine guidance, but in the shared qualities of human nature and the desperate need for reciprocity (1985, 208:51-52, emp. added).

The eminent humanistic philosopher, Will Durant, went even further when he admitted:

> By offering evolution in place of God as a cause of history, Darwin removed the theological basis of the moral code of Christendom. And the moral code that has no fear of God is very shaky. That's the condition we are in.... I don't think man is capable yet of managing social order and individual decency without fear of some supernatural being overlooking him and able to punish him (1980).

Once again, the fact remains that after everything is said and done, the atheist's second option—providing, with attending evidence, a belief system that is a "reasonable alternative"—is an unattainable goal. Enter "agnosticism."

Agnosticism

Perhaps the logical contradiction inherent in atheism (i.e., one would have to **be** God in order to **know** God does not exist) has caused many unbelievers to affirm agnosticism instead. The **agnostic** (*a*, without; *gnosis*, knowledge) is the person who says it is impossible to know if God exists, due to the fact that there simply is not enough credible evidence to warrant such a conclusion. Sproul believes that "the agnostic seeks to declare neutrality on the issue, desiring to make neither assertion nor denial of the theistic question.... The agnostic maintains that there is insufficient knowledge upon which to make an intellectual judgment about theism" (1978, pp. 19-20).

The term "agnostic" was coined by British scientist Thomas Henry Huxley, a close personal friend of Charles Darwin's and an indefatigable champion of evolution who frequently referred to himself as "Darwin's Bulldog." Huxley first introduced the word in a speech in 1869 before the Metaphysical Society. He later wrote of that occurrence:

> When I reached intellectual maturity and began to ask myself whether I was an atheist, a theist, or a pantheist; a materialist or an idealist; a Christian or a freethinker; I found that the more I learned and reflected, the less ready was the answer; until, at last, I came to the conclusion that I had neither art nor part with any of these denominations, except the last. The one thing in which most of these good people were agreed was the one thing in which I differed from them. They were quite sure they had attained a certain "gnosis"—had, more or less successfully, solved the problem of existence; while I was quite sure I had not, and had a pretty strong conviction that the problem was insoluble....
>
> This was my situation when I had the good fortune to find a place among the members of that remarkable confraternity of antagonists, long since deceased, but of green and pious memory, the Metaphysical Society. Every variety of philosophical and theological opinion was represented there, and expressed itself with entire openness; most of my colleagues were –ists of one sort or another.... So I took thought, and invented what I conceived to be the appropriate title of "agnostic." It came into my head as suggestively antithetic to the "gnostic" of Church history, who professed to know so much about the very things of which I was ignorant; and I took the earliest opportunity of parading it at our Society.... To my great satisfaction, the term took.... This is the history of the origin of the terms "agnostic" and "agnosticism" (1894, pp. 239-240, italics in orig.).

Huxley cannot be accused of inventing the term "agnostic" in a cavalier fashion. Nor can he be accused of harboring a "hidden agenda." He knew exactly what he was doing, and went about doing it in a most public fashion. He spoke often to "working class folks," frequently presenting lunchtime lectures at factories. In a letter to a friend written on March 22, 1861, he remarked: "My working men stick by me wonderfully. By Friday evening they will all be convinced that they are monkeys" (see Leonard Huxley, 1900, 1:205). He was passionate about referring to Charles Darwin as the "Newton of biology" (see Blinderman, 1957, p. 174), and did not hesitate to affirm that, so far as he was concerned,

> I really believe that the alternative is either Darwinism or nothing, for I do not know of any rational conception or theory of the organic universe which has any scientific position at all besides Mr. Darwin's.... Whatever may be the objections to his views, certainly all other theories are out of court (1896, p. 467).

Huxley worked diligently to convince those around him that agnosticism was a respectable philosophical position, and that it was quite **impossible** to know whether or not God existed. Yet he simultaneously advocated the position that it was quite **possible** to deny some theistic claims with certainty. He "knew," for example, that the Bible was not God's Word, and openly ridiculed anyone who believed it to be so. He heaped scathing rebukes upon those who believed in what he termed "the myths of Genesis," and he stated categorically that "my sole point is to get people who persist in regarding them as statements of fact to understand that they are fools" (see Leonard Huxley, 1900, 2:429).

That Huxley had in mind antagonistic views toward Judeo-Christian theism when he claimed to be "agnostic" has been made clear by those who would have no reason to be biased against him. For example, under the heading of "agnosticism," the authors of the British-produced *Encyclopaedia Britannica* wrote:

> Agnosticism both as a term and as a philosophical position gained currency through its espousal by Thomas Huxley, who seems to have coined the word "agnostic" (as opposed to "gnostic") in 1869 to designate one who repudiated traditional Judeo-Christian theism and yet disclaimed doctrinaire atheism, transcending both in order to leave such questions as the existence of God in abeyance.... But Hux-

ley's own elaboration on the term **makes it clear that this very biblical interpretation of man's relation to God was the intended polemic target of agnosticism.** The suspension of judgment on ultimate questions for which it called was thought to **invalidate Christian beliefs** about "things hoped for" and "things not seen...." Huxley himself certainly rejected as outright false—rather than as not known to be true or false—many widely popular views about God, his providence, and man's posthumous destiny... (1997a, 1:151; 1997b, 26:569, emp. added).

Rather than courageously embrace and defend atheism, Huxley opted to feign ignorance with his "I don't know, you don't know, nobody knows, and nobody **can** know" position. This cowardly compromise did not endear him to those who were quite willing to champion the more radical stance of apodictically affirming that God does not exist. In their discussion of agnosticism under the section on "religious and spiritual belief systems," the editors of *Encyclopaedia Britannica* noted that

Huxley and his associates were attacked both by enthusiastic Christian polemicists and by Friedrich Engels, the co-worker of Karl Marx, as "shame-faced atheists," **a description that is perfectly applicable to many of those who nowadays adopt the more comfortable label** (1997b, 26:569, emp. added).

The fact is, the agnostic is far from indifferent. He takes his agnosticism extremely seriously when he affirms that nothing outside of the material world can be known or proved. But agnosticism is built upon a self-defeating premise. English philosopher Herbert Spencer (also a close personal friend of Charles Darwin, the man from whom Darwin borrowed his now-popular phrase, "survival of the fittest," and popularly regarded as one of the foremost apostles of agnosticism in his day) advocated the position that just as no bird ever has been able to fly out of the heavens, so no man ever has been able to penetrate with his finite mind the veil that hides the mind of the Infinite. This inability on the part of the finite (mankind), he concluded, prevented any knowledge of the Infinite (God) reaching the finite.

Such a premise is flawed internally because it wrongly assumes that the Infinite is equally incapable of penetrating the veil —a position that reduces the term "Infinite" to absurdity. An Infinite Being that is unable to express Itself is less finite than mortals who forever are expressing themselves. And an Infinite Being that is both capable of self-expression and aware of the perplexity and needs of mortal man, yet fails to break through the veil, is less moral than mortal man. As one writer expressed it:

> What **man** would stay in shrouded silence if he were the Infinite and knew that a word from him would resolve a thousand human complexes, integrate shattered personalities, mend broken lives, bring coveted light to baffled minds, and healing peace to disturbed hearts? (Samuel, 1950, p. 14, emp. added).

To be either correct or defensible, Spencer's proposition must work **both** ways. Finite man must be unable to penetrate the veil to the Infinite, but at the same time the Infinite likewise must be unable to penetrate the veil to the finite. By definition, however, the Infinite would possess the capability of breaking through any such veil.

Further, there is an important question that begs to be asked: Will the agnostic admit that it is at least **possible** for **someone else to know** something he does not? If he is unwilling to admit this point, is he not then attributing to himself (even if inadvertently) one of the defining characteristics that theists attribute to God—omniscience? In commenting on this very point, Nelson M. Smith wrote:

> Obviously, no agnostic can speak for anyone but himself and perhaps not then. What effort has he made to know God? Has he exhausted every effort to know God? Maybe he has not been as honest with himself and with the evidence as he ought to be? Maybe he is unconsciously hiding behind a screen of "can't know" to avoid responsibility as a being made in God's image of facing his Maker? (1975, 92 [6]:6).

Smith's point is well taken. Is it not possible that the agnostic is avoiding—purposely—the evidence for the existence of God? Rather than being **unable** to know, perhaps the agnostic is **unwilling** to know. Sir Hector Hetherington, Principal Emeritus of Glasgow University, addressed this concept when he said:

> There are issues on which it is impossible to be neutral. These issues strike right down to the roots of man's existence. And while it is right that we should examine the evidence, and make sure that we have all the evidence, it is equally right that **we ourselves should be accessible to the evidence** (as quoted in Samuel, 1950, p. 29, emp. added).

The agnostic is perfectly **capable** of making himself "accessible to the evidence." The question is—**will** he? Or will he choose instead to hide "behind a screen of 'can't know'"?

Skepticism

The **skeptic** is the person who doubts there is a God. The standard dictionary definition is quite revealing when it describes a skeptic as one who holds to "the doctrine that true knowledge or knowledge in a particular area is uncertain and who has doubts concerning basic religious principles." Notice that the skeptic does not claim knowledge of God's existence is **unattainable** (as in agnosticism), but only "uncertain." However, the skeptic does not stop at mere "uncertainty." In fact, skepticism "...confidently challenges not merely religious or metaphysical knowledge but **all** knowledge claims that venture beyond immediate experience" (*Encyclopaedia Britannica*, 1997b, 26:569, emp. added). The key words here are "**immediate experience.**"

Translated into common parlance, this simply means that the skeptic is not prepared to accept **anything** that cannot be verified empirically (viz., via the scientific method). Corliss Lamont, famous twentieth-century skeptic and humanist, wrote:

The development, over the past four centuries, of a universally reliable method for attaining knowledge is a far more important achievement on the part of science than its discovery of any single truth. For once men acquire a thoroughly dependable **method** of truth-seeking, a method that can be applied to every sphere of human life and by anyone who faithfully conforms to certain directives, then they have as a permanent possession an instrument of infinite power that will serve them as long as mankind endures. Scientific method is such an instrument (1949, pp. 236-237, emp. in orig.)

Paul Kurtz, another well-known skeptic and former editor of *The Humanist* (official organ of the American Humanist Association), put it like this:

To adopt such a scientific approach unreservedly is to accept as **ultimate in all matters of fact and real existence the appeal to the evidence of experience alone; a court subordinate to no higher authority**, to be overridden by no prejudice however comfortable (1973, p. 109, emp. added).

Chet Raymo, in his book, *Skeptics and True Believers*, explained the dichotomy that exists between "Skeptics" and "True Believers" (capital letters are used throughout his book). Raymo, professor of physics and astronomy at Stonehill College in Massachusetts, has written a weekly column on science for the *Boston Globe* for more than a dozen years and was reared as a Roman Catholic. He began his book by suggesting that Skeptics and True Believers operate by different "made-up maps of the world." In chapter one he stated:

We cannot live without some sorts of make-believe in our lives. Without made-up maps of the world, life is a blooming, buzzing confusion. Some elements of our mental maps (Santa Claus...) satisfy emotional or aesthetic **inner needs**; other elements of our mental maps (hot stove, nuclear-powered stars) satisfy intellectual curiosity about the world **out there**. We get in trouble when the two kinds of maps are confused, when we objectify elements of make-believe solely on the basis of inner need.

The True Believer retains in adulthood an absolute faith in some forms of empirically unverifiable make-believe (such as astrology or the existence of immortal souls), whereas the Skeptic keeps a wary eye on firmly established facts (such as atoms). Both Skeptic and True Believer use made-up maps of the world... (1998, pp. 13-14, emp. in orig.).

Raymo then went on to ask:

Is one map as good as any other? Since all knowledge is constructed, can the choice between two contradictory maps ...be a matter of personal or political expediency? Not unless we are willing to erect partitions between what we **know to be true on the basis of unambiguous, reproducible evidence** and what we merely **wish to be true**. Apparently, many of us are willing to do just that (1998, p. 14, emp. added).

With his strict dichotomy between the Skeptic (a person who **knows** about such things as atoms and nuclear-powered stars—"on the basis of unambiguous, reproducible evidence") and the True Believer (a person who **believes** in such things as Santa Claus, astrology, and an immortal soul—in spite of the evidence) firmly in place, Raymo then spent the remainder of his book laying out the Skeptic's case against: (a) the existence of God; (b) the Genesis account of creation; (c) the occurrence of biblical miracles; (d) etc. Eventually, however, he was forced to admit:

The forces that nudge us toward True Belief are pervasive and well-nigh irresistible. Supernatural faith systems provide a degree of emotional security that skepticism cannot provide. Who among us would **not** prefer that there exists a divine parent who has our best interest at heart? Who among us would **not** prefer to believe that we will live forever? Skepticism, on the other hand, offers only uncertainty and doubt.... Science cannot rule out heaven and hell because they are beyond the reach of empirical investigation (1998, pp. 5,77, emp. in orig.).

Thus, in the end the skeptic does not say he **cannot** know that God exists. Rather, he says he **doubts** that God exists because He cannot be seen, felt, measured, weighed, or probed by the scientific method. Thirty-four years before Chet Raymo wrote about "Skeptics and True Believers," George Gaylord Simpson, the late evolutionist of Harvard, wrote: "It is inherent in any definition of science that statements that cannot be checked by observation are not really saying anything..." (1964, p. 769). Simply put, the point is this: If science cannot deal with something, that "something" either does not exist (worst-case scenario) or is completely unimportant (best-case scenario). Welcome to the make-believe world of the skeptic in which science reigns supreme and a cavalier attitude toward all things non-empirical rules the day.

But what about those concepts that, although non-empirical and therefore unobservable via the scientific method, nevertheless are recognized to exist, and are admitted to be of critical importance to the entire human race—concepts like love, sorrow, joy, altruism, etc.? Arlie Hoover accurately assessed the situation in which the skeptic finds himself in regard to the existence of such items when he wrote:

> Why does the scientific method reject subjective factors, emotions, feelings? Simply because it is not convenient! Because the method will not allow you to deal with the immense complexity of reality. The scientist, therefore, selects from the whole of experience only those elements that can be weighed, measured, numbered, or which lend themselves to mathematical treatment....
>
> This is a fallacy we call **Reductionism**. You commit the Reductive Fallacy when you select a portion of a complex entity and say the whole is merely that portion. You do this when you say things like: love is nothing but sex, man is just an animal, music is nothing but sound waves, art is nothing but color.... When it gets down to the real serious questions of life—origin, purpose, destiny, meaning, morality—science is silent....
>
> If science can't handle morality, aesthetics, and religion that only proves that the scientific method was reductive in the first place. Sir Arthur Eddington once used a famous analogy to illustrate this reductionism. He told of a fisherman who concluded from his fishing experiences with a certain net

that "no creature of the sea is less than two inches long." Now this disturbed many of his colleagues and they demurred, pointing out that many sea creatures are under two inches and they just slipped through the two-inch holes in the net. But the ichthyologist was unmoved: "What my net can't catch ain't fish," he pontificated, and then he scornfully accused his critics of having pre-scientific, medieval, metaphysical prejudices.

Scientific reductionism or "Scientism"—as it is often called—is similar to this fisherman with the special net. Since the strict empirical scientist can't "catch" or "grasp" such qualitative things like freedom, morality, aesthetics, mind, and God, he concludes that they don't exist. But they have just slipped through his net. They have been slipping through his net all the way from Democritus to B.F. Skinner to Carl Sagan (1981, p. 6, emp. in orig.).

In speaking of skepticism and its offspring of humanism, Sir Julian Huxley wrote: "It will have **nothing to do with absolutes**, including absolute truth, absolute morality, absolute perfection and absolute authority" (1964, pp. 73-74, emp. added). To that list, one might add absolute joy, absolute love, absolute freedom, absolute peace, etc. The skeptic has paid a high price for his scientism—the rejection and abandonment of some of the human race's most important, valuable, worthwhile, and cherished, concepts. Why? In order to be able to say: I **doubt** that God exists!

Infidelity

The **infidel** is the person who not only refuses to believe in God himself, but also is intolerant of, and actively opposed to, those who do. A study of human history provides a veritable plethora of men and women who made quite a name for themselves via their public display of infidelity. In the third century A.D., for example, Porphyry wrote a fifteen-volume series (*Against Christians*) in which he sought to lay bare alleged contradictions between the Old and New Testaments and to document how the apostles had contradicted themselves. He excoriated the book of

Daniel, and charged Jesus with equivocation and inconsistency. He was recognized widely as one of the most celebrated enemies of God the world ever has known. McClintock and Strong have suggested that he "...became the most determined of heathen polemics the world ever beheld or Christianity ever encountered" (1879, 8:422).

Another infidel of the ancient past whose name is associated with vitriolic opposition to God was the Frenchman Voltaire. Beginning in 1765, he attacked Christianity with viciousness and vigor. He began with what today would be styled "higher criticism," by which he brought into question the authenticity and reliability of the Bible. He then alleged chronological contradictions in the narratives of the Old Testament. He challenged as incorrect many of the messianic prophecies of the Old Testament, and he stoutly denied any such things as miracles and the efficacy of prayer. He once boasted: "It took 12 men to originate the Christian religion, but it will take but one to eliminate it. Within fifty years from now the only Bible will be in museums" (as quoted in Key, 1982, p. 2). [Interestingly, not long after his death, the Geneva Bible Society purchased Voltaire's house and used his printing presses to print French New Testaments.]

David Hume, born in 1711 in Scotland, attacked the idea of the immortality of the soul and placed the origin of religion on par with the existence of things like elves and fairies. But he no doubt is most famous for his essay, "Of Miracles," which was tucked away in his work, *Enquiry Concerning Human Understanding*, published in 1748. The essay itself consisted of scarcely more than 20 pages, but concluded that from what we know about the laws of nature a miracle simply cannot occur. The treatise went on to suggest that historical testimony regarding miracles is specious, and never could be strong enough to override more important scientific considerations. For Hume, there was **no** evidence strong enough to prove that miracles actually had taken place. His attack upon biblical miracles had serious consequences upon religion generally, and Christianity specifically. Even today many refuse to believe in God because of David Hume's arguments.

One of Christianity's most ardent opponents in the 1800s was Joseph Ernest Renan. Born in 1823, he was a French historian who rejected any supernatural content in religion. In 1860, he wrote *The Life of Jesus*, in which he repudiated all supernatural elements in Christ's life and ministry. The book was a frontal assault upon the personal deity of Christ and received much attention throughout Europe, assuring Renan of instant fame. He subsequently authored a book on the apostle Paul, and a five-volume set on the history of Israel. Today his place in history as an infidel has been sealed as a result of his strident attacks upon Jesus.

In more recent times, one of the most vicious attacks upon God, Christ, and the Bible was spearheaded by Robert Ingersoll. Born in Dresden, New York in 1833, he set up his law practice in Peoria, Illinois in 1858, and eventually was appointed as that state's Attorney General. Madalyn Murray O'Hair, while still director of American Atheists in Austin, Texas, once characterized Ingersoll as "...a superb egotist. And, he engaged in more than one drunken public brawl.... Not withstanding all of the anomalies of his character, he was magnificent when he did get going on either religion or the church..." (1983, p. vi).

In *The Atheist Syndrome*, John Koster has suggested concerning Ingersoll that "what he hated was organized religion" (1989, p. 123). Shortly after Ingersoll went on the lecture circuit around 1877, he began to include in his repertoire such topics as "Heretics and Heresies" and "Ghosts"—both of which were undisguised attacks upon religion generally, and Christianity specifically. By 1878, he had expanded his lectures to include "Hell" and "Some Mistakes of Moses," both of which were favorites of atheists of his day. He died in 1899, having established his reputation both as an atheist and an influential infidel.

John Dewey was born in Vermont in 1859. He completed a doctorate at Johns Hopkins and in 1884 began teaching at the University of Michigan. In 1894, he was appointed chairman of the department of philosophy, psychology, and education at the University of Chicago. In 1904, he left Chicago and moved to Columbia University where he remained until his retirement in 1930. More than any other individual before or since, Dewey's views have altered American educational processes. Durant wrote: "...there is hardly a school in America that has not felt his influence" (1961, p. 390). Why did he have such an impact? Durant went on to explain:

> What separates Dewey is the undisguised completeness with which he accepts the evolution theory. Mind as well as body is to him an organ evolved, in the struggle for existence, from lower forms. His starting point in every field is Darwinian.... Things are to be explained, then, not by supernatural causation, but by their place and function in the environment. Dewey is frankly naturalistic... (1961, p. 391).

Dewey was a prolific writer, and eventually authored *A Common Faith* in which he discussed religion (and in which his infidelity was brought into full view). He made it clear that "he wished at all costs to be scientific; for him the processes of science are the most obvious and the most successful methods of knowing. Therefore if science neglects something, the something is nothing" (Clark, 1957, p. 519). Because he viewed religion as "unscientific," he therefore considered it to be "nothing," which was why he vehemently opposed religion of any kind and insisted upon the teaching of organic evolution as fact, not theory. In his writings he stressed that "moral laws" were neither absolute nor inviolable and unabashedly advocated situation ethics. Dewey died in 1952, having altered forever the landscape of American education and having ensured his reputation as one of the chief infidels of the twentieth century. Had he lived a few years longer, he would have seen his ideas on the naturalistic origin and basis of all things take hold in a way that perhaps even he never dreamed.

Madalyn Murray O'Hair was the most famous atheist/infidel in America for more than three-and-a-half decades. Her public saga began in 1963 when a suit to remove prayer from public schools was heard before the United States Supreme Court. Although the suit (in which Mrs. O'Hair was only a secondary litigant) originally had been filed in the name of Philadelphia Unitarian, Ed Schempp, she took over the battle and ultimately was victorious in the landmark decision of *Murray v. Curlett*. A writer in *Time* magazine described her as

> ...a heavy woman with a strong voice and a jaw who even in repose resembled, as author Lawrence Wright once observed, "a bowling ball looking for new pins to scatter." She was an Army veteran and a law-school graduate and a big talker. Most important, she was an atheist.... "I love a good fight," she said. "I guess fighting God and God's spokesmen is sort of the ultimate, isn't it?" (Van Biema, 1997, pp. 56,57).

She was the star of the first episode of Phil Donahue's television talk show. She filed lawsuits at what one journalist called "a near pathological level of pugnacity" for 32 years (Van Biema, 1997, p. 57). And once, while watching a female orangutan on television, she quipped, "The Virgin just made another appearance" (as quoted in Van Biema, p. 57).

In 1965, having worn out her welcome with state and local authorities in Maryland and Hawaii, she settled in Austin, Texas and formed the Society of Separationists, later adding the Atheist Centre in America and several other satellite groups. In the 1980s, she enjoyed a heyday as she ruled over her pet project that came to be known simply as "American Atheists," from which she published her pratings against God via books, posters, and bumper stickers (e.g., "Apes Evolved From Creationists"). She would debate anyone, anywhere, anytime on the existence of God and the "atrocities" of organized religion.

In fact, in the late 1970s, while I was serving as a professor in the College of Veterinary Medicine at Texas A&M University, I attended a debate she conducted with Bob Harrington, a denominational preacher from New Orleans known popularly as "the chaplain of Bourbon Street." Mrs. O'Hair was (and I say this not in any derogatory sense, but only from personal observation as a member of the audience) unkempt, haggard, slovenly, and bitter. During the course of the debate, she cursed wildly (frequently taking God's name in vain), belittled the audience for its "obvious" lack of intelligence, and mocked her opponent. She was on the lookout for, and seized, every possible opportunity to berate God and anyone who, in her considered opinion, was "stupid enough" to believe in Him. Little wonder that in 1964 *Life* magazine headlined her as "the most hated woman in America." Bruce Lockerbie wrote regarding Mrs. O'Hair:

> When we begin to speak of O'Hair and others like her, we turn directly into the face of aggressively militant **disbelief**. Here is no lady-like apologist, no grandmotherly disputant; for O'Hair, the cause is nothing short of all-out war (1998, p. 231).

Then suddenly, without warning, she disappeared—vanished without a trace. On August 28, 1995 workers at the American Atheists building came to work, only to find a note taped to the front door that read: "We've been called out on an emergency basis, and we'll call you when we get back." But she (along with her son Jon and his daughter Robin who disappeared with her) never called, and never has been back. Curiously, about the same time over $600,000 turned up missing from the treasury of American Atheists. In 1995, tax forms submitted by the United Secularists of America (one of American Atheists' satellite groups) documented a $612,000 decrease in net assets and admitted:

> The $612,000...represents the value of the United Secularists of America's assets believed to be in the possession of Jon Murray, former Secretary. The whereabouts of Jon Murray and these assets have not been known since September 1995 and is not known to the organization at this time (as quoted in Van Biema, 1997, p. 59).

[In April 1999, Ron Barrier, national spokesman for American Atheists, announced that the group was moving its headquarters from Austin, Texas to Cranford, New Jersey, stating that "the Northeast is much more progressive than the South..." (*Montgomery Advertiser*, 1999, D-3). On Sunday, April 4, 1999 a dedication ceremony was held for the new offices in Cranford.]

It can be said without fear of contradiction that "the most hated woman in America"—who had made it her life's goal to oppose God—did not live **up** to anyone's expectations, but undeniably lived **down** to the level of her self-professed atheism. The history of infidelity, only a brief overview of which I have examined here, documents all too well that she has not been alone. In his novel, *The Brothers Karamazov*, Russian novelist Fyodor Dostoevsky had one of his characters, Ivan, comment that if there is no God, everything is permitted. French atheist and existential philosopher, Jean Paul Sartre, opined:

> Everything is indeed permitted if God does not exist, and man is in consequence forlorn, for he cannot find anything to depend upon either within or outside himself.... Nor, on the other hand, if God does not exist, are we provided with any values or commands that could legitimize our behavior (1961, p. 485).

As essayist G.K. Chesterton once observed: "When men cease to believe in God, they do not believe in **nothing**; they believe in **anything**" (as quoted in Bales, 1967, p. 133, emp. added).

Deism

The concept of deism (from the Latin *deus*, god) had its beginnings among writers in seventeenth-century England, beginning with Edward Herbert (1581-1648) who later became the first Baron Herbert of Cherbury and who often is recognized as the "father of deism." In his 1624 book, *De Veritate* (*On Truth*), Lord Herbert laid out five basic principles of deism: "(1) The being of God; (2) that he is to be worshipped; (3) that piety and moral virtue are the chief parts of worship; (4) that God will pardon our faults on repentance; and, (5) that there is a future state of rewards and punishment" (see McClintock and Strong, 1879, 2: 730). In the second edition of that work (1645), Herbert expanded his ideas as he dealt with the foundations of religion and critiqued the idea of direct revelation from God. That same year, he further elaborated his views in the book, *De Causis Errorum* (*Concerning the Causes of Errors*). An additional work, *De Religione Gentilium* (*The Religion of the Gentiles*) was published posthumously in 1663. He urged a quick and permanent abandonment of the idea that God intervened supernaturally in man's world in any way.

Herbert's views were propagated by a number of influential British writers such as his chief disciple, Charles Blount (1654-1693), Anthony Collins (1676-1729), Thomas Woolston (1670-1731), Matthew Tindal (1655-1733), and Peter Annet (1693-1769), who was the last of the old-line British deists. In the eighteenth century, deism flourished in France. In fact, "English deism strongly influenced later French deism and skepticism, of which Diderot and Voltaire are notable examples" (Geisler, 1976, p. 165). Shortly thereafter, deism spread to Germany and held sway in Europe for a hundred years. Norman Geisler has added:

> Along the way there were many philosophical figures who may not technically qualify as deists but who nonetheless gave impetus to and provided arguments for the movement. Bacon's scientific approach, John Locke's empiricism, and David Hume's skepticism about miracles definitely aided the deistic cause (1976, p. 152).

Eventually deism spread to early colonial America as well. The editors of *Encyclopaedia Britannica* noted:

> By the end of the 18th century, Deism had become a dominant religious attitude among intellectual and upper class Americans.... The first three presidents of the United States also held deistic convictions, as is amply evidenced in their correspondence (1997b, 26:569).

The evidence sustains such an assessment.

> In America deism flourished after it had declined in England. Thomas Jefferson, Benjamin Franklin, and Thomas Paine are classed as deists.... Perhaps more than anywhere else in the United States, deistic tendencies of naturalism and Biblical criticism have lived on in modernistic or liberal Protestantism... (Geisler, 1976, pp. 165-166).

But why was such a system necessary? Basically deism came into existence as men attempted to work around the contradictions and internal inconsistencies posed by atheism and agnosticism. The atheist was unable to disprove God's existence, and the agnostic was forced to admit that while **he** might not be able to **know** that God exists, someone else certainly might possess such knowledge. Enter deism.

> The best way out of the dilemmas posed by atheism and agnosticism would appear to be the following: let us say that there is a God. This God created the world. He issued to the world a moral law, a code of behavior which all of His creatures are supposed to follow. God will someday judge His creatures on how well they obeyed His commandments. In the meantime He does not interfere with His creation. He made it the way He wanted it to be, and He will not contradict His own will. For the moment, we worship God and try to live by His law, but we must not expect Him to do supernatural things for us (Corduan, 1993, p. 90).

What, then, are the exact tenets of deism? Truth be told, at times those tenets are not at all easy to decipher.

> In the late seventeenth and in the eighteenth century more than a few thinkers came to be called deists or called themselves deists. These men held a number of related views, but not all held every doctrine in common. John Locke, for example, did not reject the idea of revelation, but he did insist that human reason was to be used to judge it. Some deists, like Voltaire, were hostile to Christianity; some, like Locke, were not. Some believed in the immortality of the soul; some did not. Some believed God left his creation to function on its own; some believed in providence. Some believed in a personal God; others did not. So deists were much less united on basic issues than were theists (Sire, 1988, p. 50).

By way of summary, however, it may be said that the **deist** begrudgingly acknowledges that God exists, and even grants that God created the Universe and its inhabitants. But deism insists that since His initial miraculous act of creation, God has had nothing whatsoever to do with either the Universe or mankind. As the editors of *Encyclopaedia Britannica* have observed:

> At times in the 19th and 20th centuries, the word Deism was used theologically in contradistinction to theism, the belief in an immanent God who actively intervenes in the affairs of men. In this sense Deism was represented as the view of those who reduced the role of God to a mere act of creation in accordance with rational laws discovered by man and held that, after the original act, God virtually withdrew and refrained from interfering in the processes of nature and the ways of man (1997b, 26:567).

The basic idea behind deism often is discussed and clarified via the analogy of a clock, the idea being that God created the clock, wound it up, and then walked away to leave it operating on its own. In his book, *The Universe Next Door*, James W. Sire titled his chapter on deism, "The Clockwork Universe," and commented that according to the deist "God is thus not immanent, not fully personal, not sovereign over human affairs, not providential.... God is not interested in individual men and women or even whole peoples" (1988, pp. 50,56). The God of deism therefore has been called a "hermit God" (Dickson, 1979, 121 [8]:118), an "absentee landlord" (Brown, 1984, p. 47), and a "God in absentia" (Coats, 1989, p. 61). The deist's position is not that God **cannot** perform miracles; rather it is that God **will not** perform miracles because "according to deism, it is contrary to God's nature to do miracles.... In deism God and the supernatural are considered to be incompatible" (Corduan, 1993, p. 91).

Such a position inevitably leads to the following. First, deism rejects both the triune nature of the Godhead and the deity of Christ. Geisler and Brooks assessed the matter by suggesting that deists

...believe that God never specially intervenes in the world to help mankind. Since this also means that Jesus was not God (that would be a miracle), there is no reason for them to believe that God is a Trinity. The idea of three Persons in one nature (the Trinity) is to them just bad math (1990, p. 40; parenthetical comments in orig.).

Or, as Hoover has noted: "Deists believed in a Supreme Being, but he was only one in number. They denied the doctrines of Trinity and Incarnation. Jesus Christ was merely a great moral teacher" (1976, p. 12). Thus, the deist denies "any supernatural redemptive act in history" (Harrison, 1966, p. 162).

Second, deism rejects the idea that God has given a special revelation of Himself in the Bible. For God to reveal Himself by speaking directly to man would be a miracle—an intervention into man's world. This is something the deist is not prepared to accept. Observation of the general revelation that God has left of Himself in nature, says the deist, is sufficient for understanding the Creator and His desires for mankind.

> What did a typical deist deny? In one word: **intervention**.... God didn't need to reveal anything about himself in a holy book like the Bible or the Koran. Nature itself is the only revelation God needs. A rational man could find out all that he needed to know about God from nature... (Hoover, 1976, p. 13, emp. in orig.).

In summarizing the aversion of the deist to the miraculous, Roger Dickson noted that "the principle point of concern here is the deist's denial of the inspiration of the Bible and miracles. If God does not intervene in the natural world, then both are impossible" (1979, p. 118).

Third, deism advocates that human reason alone is all man needs to understand God and His laws for humankind.

> Deism...refers to what can be called natural religion, the acceptance of a certain body of religious knowledge that is inborn in every person or that can be acquired by the use of reason, as opposed to knowledge acquired through either revelation or the teaching of any church...(Encyclopaedia Britannica, 1997b, 26:567).

Sir Peter Medawar put it this way: "The 17th-century doctrine of the **necessity** of reason was slowly giving way to a belief in the **sufficiency** of reason" (1969, p. 438). Without special revelation from God (a miracle), deism had no choice but to advocate that **reason alone was sufficient**.

Fourth, deism rejects the notions of a prayer-hearing/prayer-answering God and a God Who works in men's lives through divine providence. As Hoover observed: "If you deny revelation you must also sweep out miracle, prayer, and providence. **Any** tampering with nature and her perfect laws would imply that nature had a defect" (1976, p. 13, emp. in orig.). Coats lamented:

> With his concept of God, there is no possible way for the deist to believe in the providence of God. Since God has taken a long journey and is "**at rest**," He leaves the affairs of men and nations to tick alone, as would the pendulum of a clock. There is no reason to pray to a deistic god for the system is completely fatalistic (1989, p. 61, emp. in orig.).

What response may be offered to deism? First, deism's flawed view of God's inability to work miracles must be addressed. Corduan has reasoned as follows:

> Now we can see that deism is actually irrational.... If God can perform the miracle of creation, there is no good reason why He cannot do other miracles. Thus deism has an inconsistency at its core. Two affirmations are at the heart of deism: (1) God performed the miracle of creation; and (2) God does not perform miracles. If you are a deist, you must believe both of them, and yet these affirmations cannot both be true. Therefore deism is not a believable worldview. It founders on the criterion of consistency (1993, pp. 91-92).

In speaking to this same point, Geisler added:

> Since God performed the miracle of creation *ex nihilo* (from nothing), it follows from the very nature and power of this kind of God that other lesser miracle are possible. Walking on water is little problem for a God who created water to begin with. To make a human through a female ovum (virgin birth) is not difficult for a God who made a world

from nothing. And multiplying loaves is surely not a greater feat than creating matter in the first place. In short, it is self-defeating to admit the miracle of creation and to deny that other miracles are possible (1976, p. 169; parenthetical comments in orig.).

Second, if the deist believes supernatural Creation occurred, he cannot deny the only divine source of knowledge concerning that Creation—special revelation.

> The deistic arguments intended to eliminate the basis for belief in a supernatural revelation apply equally as well to elimination of the deistic belief in creation.... If the Bible cannot be trusted to teach one doctrine then there is no grounds for believing the other one is true.... Hence, the deist defeats his own case against revelation when he accepts from revelation the doctrine of creation (Geisler, 1976, p. 170).

Third, since God created the laws of the Universe, and since those laws are contingent upon God for their very existence, there is no good reason why an omnipotent God could not set aside those laws for the benefit of mankind. Furthermore, would not a God concerned enough to create humans likewise be concerned enough to intervene on their behalf on occasion—especially if they had fallen into grave (spiritual) danger? Geisler has suggested:

> "You have made your own bed, lie in it" is something less than the attitude a good Creator ought to have. If he had enough love and concern for man to create him, then it would seem to be most compatible with such a nature to believe that God would miraculously intervene to help him if he were in need. And surely a God strong enough to create the world is strong enough to help it. The laws of creation are not inviolable; they are created and contingent. And what is created and contingent can be laid aside if need be for the moral good of man. Hence, the nature of God, even as conceived by deists, would be compatible with miraculous intervention into the natural world when the situation calls for it (1976, p. 170).

As Corduan has said: "God is not just a disinterested spectator, but He is deeply interested in the moral progress His creatures are making" (1993, p. 90). God is not merely a "Master Universe Mechanic." He also is personal—a concept even deists accept. Is it not reasonable, then, to suggest that this personal Creator would desire communication between Himself and His creation— especially if the creation had been made "in His image"? Geisler has remarked:

> Miraculous commerce between the personal Creator and the persons created would not only be possible, it would seem to be most probable. If the desire to have personal communication between the supernatural and the natural realm flows from God as personal, then not to perform miracles of personal communication (viz., revelation) would show God to be something less than perfectly personal. It is inconsistent to disallow a personal communication from the supernatural realm to the natural realm once one has admitted God is personal (1976, p. 170).

Fourth, the idea that human reason alone is an adequate guide for mankind, and that the "natural world" can provide him with all that he needs to know in regard to behavior, ethics, response to God, etc., is severely flawed. As Hoover noted:

> Deistic thinkers seldom agree on what God is like, even though he is supposed to be the same to all minds who simply reason properly. If you don't believe me, try it for yourself. Compare the Gods of (say) Aristotle, Spinoza, and Tom Paine. You'll be depressed at the different pictures of God that reason alone comes up with in different men! (1976, pp. 14-15, parenthetical item in orig.).

When man exalts "reason alone" as the final standard, and limits his knowledge of God to whatever he can discern from the natural world around him, he is destined to fail. As Sire has explained:

> In some ways, we can say that limiting knowledge about God to general revelation is like finding that eating eggs for breakfast makes the morning go well—and then eating **only** eggs for breakfast (and maybe lunch and dinner too) for

the rest of one's life (which now unwittingly becomes rather shortened!). To be sure theism assumes that we can know something about God from nature. But it also holds that there is much **more to know** than can be known that way and that there are **other ways to know** (1988, pp. 49-50, parenthetical comments and emp. in orig.).

Consider such an admonition as it relates to the deist's belief that human ethics and morals may be fashioned by mere "reason alone" based on the "natural world." Hoover has commented:

Especially puerile was the deistic belief that you could establish an ethical code by mere reason based only on nature. Which part of nature do we consult for this moral standard? What animal gives us the norm? Some spiders eat their mate after sexual intercourse—should we humans imitate this example? If not, which animal shall we follow? (1976, p. 14).

If, according to deism, the Universe is both normal and perfect, and nature is God's complete revelation of Himself, then obviously both would reveal what is right. This leads inevitably to the position that

...God, being the omnipotent Creator, becomes responsible **for everything as it is**. This world must then reflect either what God wants or what he is like. Ethically, this leads to the position expressed by Alexander Pope [in volume one, line 294 of his work, *Essay on Man*—BT]: "One truth is clear, **whatever is, is right**." This position really ends in destroying ethics. If whatever is, is right, then there is no evil. Good becomes indistinguishable from evil.... Or, worse luck, there must be no **good** at all. For without the ability to distinguish, there can be neither one nor the other, neither good nor evil. Ethics disappears (Sire, 1988, pp. 54-55, first emp. added, last two in orig.).

Fifth, deism became the easily crossed bridge from theism to out-and-out naturalism—the view that there is no God and that "nature" is all that exists. Sire summed up this fact when he wrote:

Deism did not prove to be a very stable world view. Historically it held sway over the intellectual world of France and England briefly from the late seventeenth into the first half of the eighteenth century. **Preceded by theism, it was followed by naturalism** (1988, pp. 56-57, emp. added).

Roger Dickson has pointed out that for many of its adherents, "deism was the first step toward naturalism" (1979, 121[8]:118). In his monumental work, *Does God Exist?*, Hans Kung summarized the situation as follows:

> This Deism, not accepted by theology, which still needed God in the physical world...now developed consistently into a **scientific atheism**, which did not need God either physically for the explanation of the world or even morally for the conduct of life (1980, p. 91, emp. in orig.).

Today, it is rare to find a genuine deist. I mention the concept here, however, not merely from a historical perspective, but also to document the end result of accepting it. As Kung poignantly noted, deism "developed consistently into a **scientific atheism**, which did not need God."

Pantheism

In the above section on deism, Hans Kung observed that eventually deism led to scientific atheism. However, he also noted that it did not necessarily follow a direct path. He went on to say:

> Almost imperceptibly, over a long period, a significant change had come about in the intellectual climate and with it also a change in the understanding of God: **away from the deism of the Enlightenment to a basically pantheistic attitude** (1980, p. 133, emp. in orig.).

I now would like to discuss the concept of pantheism in this context.

Both theists and deists hold to a view which suggests that God is "out there." In other words, He is **transcendent**—i.e., beyond the world. Pantheism (*pan*, all; *theos*, God), on the other hand, teaches that God is "in here." He is not in the least transcendent, but merely **immanent**—i.e., in the world. Put in the bluntest possible terms, "God and the world are so closely intertwined that you cannot tell them apart" (Corduan, 1993, p. 92). The central tenet of pantheism is that all is God and God is all. The seventeenth-century philosopher, Baruch Spinoza (1632-1677), was an outspoken advocate of the concept. In commenting on Spinoza's influence in this regard, Kung wrote:

> Spinoza's God does not live apart from the universe: God is in the world and the world is in God. Nature is a particular way in which God himself exists; human consciousness is a particular way in which God himself thinks. The individual self and all finite things are not autonomous substances but only modifications of the **one and only divine substance.** God, then, all in all—[is] a purely immanent, not a transcendent God (1980, p. 133, emp. in orig.).

While pantheism long has been associated with eastern religions such as Hinduism, Taoism, and some forms of Buddhism, in recent years it has made serious inroads into western thinking, as is evident from the teachings of the Christian Science religion, Scientology, and certain others. Its best-known public forum today is the teachings of the New Age movement, most noticeably the writings of Oscar-winning actress, Shirley MacLaine. In her book, *Out on a Limb*, she told of her discussions with a friend by the name of Kevin Ryerson who allegedly was able to "channel" John—a disembodied spirit from the days of Jesus' earthly sojourn. Once, when Ms. MacLaine was speaking with "John," he allegedly said to her: "[Y]our soul is a metaphor for God.... **You** are God. **You** know you are divine" (1983, pp. 209, emp. in orig.). In addressing what she refers to as her "higher self" in her book, *Dancing in the Light*, MacLaine said: "**I am God**, because all energy is plugged in to the same source. We are each aspects of that source. We are all part of God. We are individualized reflections of the God source. God is us and we are God" (1991, p. 339, emp. added). In her 1989 book, *Going Within*, she wrote: "I, for example, do a silent mantra with each of my hatha yoga poses. I hold each yoga position for twenty seconds and internally chant, 'I am God in Light'" (1989, p. 57).

In the book he authored refuting MacLaine's views, *Out on a Broken Limb*, lawyer F. LaGard Smith stated:

> The heart and soul of the New Age movement, which Ms. MacLaine embraces along with her reincarnation ideas, is nothing less than **self-deification**.... But it really shouldn't be all that surprising. All we had to do was put the equation together: We are One; God is One; therefore, we are God. The cosmic conjugation is: I am God, you are God, we are God.... Surely if someone tells herself repeatedly that she is God, it won't be long before she actually believes it! (1986, pp. 178,179-180,181, emp. in orig.).

In trying to comprehend the thinking behind such concepts, it is essential to understand that although pantheism sounds like a theory about the cosmos, actually it is a theory about self—the individual human being. Since each individual is a part of the Universe, since God is "in" the Universe and the Universe is "in" God, and since each individual shares the "divine nature" of the Universe, each individual **is God**. When Shirley MacLaine stands on the sands of the beach and yells out loud, "I am God" (1983), she literally means just what she says!

There are different varieties of pantheism, to be sure. In his book, *Christian Apologetics*, Norman Geisler has devoted an entire chapter to a discussion of these variants (1976, pp. 173-192). But perhaps one of the most important threads running through each is the identification of God with the world. Winfried Corduan addressed this topic when he observed:

> In this worldview, God and the world are identical, not just in the sense of identical twins, who merely resemble each other strongly, but in the sense of being one and the same thing. The words "world" and "God" are then used as two different expressions for one thing (1993, p. 92).

Think about the implications of such a view. If pantheism is correct, then there no longer is a need for we humans to "look beyond ourselves" for solutions to whatever problems it is that plague us. Instead, we simply may "look within." We, being God, are our own source of truth. We, being God, can decide what is right and what is wrong. All the power that we need to cope with life and its vagaries lies within the untapped reservoir of human potential we call "self."

Sounds good—at first glance. But carry this kind of thinking to its logical end. First, if we are God, sin and its associated concept of redemption become unnecessary. Second, because God is not beyond the world but in it, there can be no miracles (as we normally would employ that term—i.e., **supernatural** events). While there may be **supernormal** events (e.g., channelings, healings, the ability to resist pain while walking on a bed of hot coals, etc.), since these things are not accomplished by any power outside the Universe, but instead are the result of people realizing and employing their divine potential, then "miracles" do not and cannot occur. Third, in pantheism there is neither need of, nor allowance for, divine providence. The consensus of pantheism is that, since God is all and all is God, and since God is good, then anything evil must not, and cannot, really exist. After all, if it existed, it would be God. As the pantheists themselves put it:

> ...Every action, under certain circumstances and for certain people, may be a stepping-stone to spiritual growth, if it is done in a spirit of detachment. All good and evil are relative to the individual point of growth.... But, in the highest sense, there can be neither good nor evil (Prabhavananda and Isherwood, 1972, p. 140).

If, "in the highest sense" neither good nor evil exists, then obviously mankind has no need of providence. Why should man want God to "look out for" him if there is no evil with which he has to be concerned and if he is all-powerful himself? Fourth, when pantheism is reduced to its basic, core concepts, it becomes clear that God does not have a personality, as depicted within Scripture; thus, He is not a "person" but an "it." As Geisler observed: "In the highest and absolute sense God is **neither personal nor conscious**. The Absolute and Supreme is not a He but an It"

(1976, p. 185, emp. in orig.). Erich Sauer wrote of how pantheism "...teaches the immanence of the Deity in the universe but denies the personality of God" (1962, p. 163). Fifth, pantheism advocates the view that there is one absolute, unchanging reality—God—and that humans, given time and proper teaching, can come to the realization that they, too, are God. This is exactly the position that Shirley MacLaine takes in her books, *Out on Limb*, *Going Within*, and *Dancing in the Light*. Eventually, she was able to stand on the sands of the beach and proclaim, "I am God!"

How should Christians respond to the concept of pantheism? First, we must point out that the pantheistic concept of "all is God and God is all" is wrong because it attempts to sustain itself via a contradiction. In logic, one of the fundamental laws of human thought is the basic Law of Contradiction, which, stated succinctly, says: "Nothing can both be and not be" (Jevons, 1928, p. 117). Aristotle, expressed it more fully when he said: "That the same thing should at the same time both be and not be for the same person and in the same respect is impossible" (see Arndt, 1955, p. x). Another ramification of the Law of Contradiction is the concept that "nothing can have at the same time and at the same place contradictory and inconsistent qualities" (Jevons, p. 118). A door may be open, or a door may be shut, but the same door may not be both open and shut at the same time. The entire system of pantheism, however, sustains itself via a logical contradiction. Corduan commented on this as follows:

> Pantheism is built around a contradiction, and a contradiction can never be true. No matter how spiritual or profound or enticing a message may appear it must be false if it contradicts itself. The primary contradiction of pantheism is that the two descriptions "world" and "God" are irreconcilably mutually exclusive.... Who (or what) is God? Pantheists agree that God is **infinite**, which includes that He is eternal, omnipotent, unchanging, and so forth. This understanding of God is at the heart of pantheism.... In pantheism, God is infinite.... What is the world? The world is **fi-**

nite. It is temporal, limited, and changeable. Yet pantheism tells us that this description of reality as finite world and the description of reality as infinite God are both true. Can this be? Can something be both finite and infinite? The answer is clearly no.... The point here is not to ridicule but to show that the pantheists' attempts to identify God and the world with each other cannot work. **It is not just too hard, it is impossible**. There is a categorical distinction between God and the world (1993, pp. 93,94, emp. added).

This is where the Law of Contradiction sets itself against pantheism. If it is true that "nothing can have at the same time and at the same place contradictory and inconsistent qualities" (and it is!), then one cannot say that God and the world are identical while at the same time asserting that God is infinite and the world finite. If words mean anything, such a dichotomy is the death knell to pantheism.

Second, we need to stress that, so far as God's Word is concerned, everything is not "one." The Bible clearly distinguishes between two different realms: the material and the spiritual. Solomon wrote: "Then the dust will return to the earth as it was, and the spirit will return to God who gave it" (Ecclesiastes 12:7). The writer of the book of Hebrews said: "Furthermore, we have had human fathers who corrected us, and we paid them respect. Shall we not much more readily be in subjection to the Father of spirits and live?" (12:9). Jesus was even more explicit when He affirmed that "God is Spirit" and then later stated: "Handle me and see, for a spirit does not have flesh and bones as you see I have" (John 4:24; Luke 24:39).

The Bible not only teaches that there is a distinction between the material and spiritual realms, but also notes that there is an essential difference among the various orders of creation. The Genesis account of creation reports how God created plants, animals, and men separately. Thus, in a very real sense it is erroneous to speak of man as "one" with nature—for he most certainly is not. Paul wrote: "All flesh is not the same flesh, but there is one kind of flesh of men, another flesh of beasts, another of fish, and another of birds" (1 Corinthians 15:39). Far from "all being one," nature's inhabitants actually were created by God to fulfill separate roles. The idea that "all is one" simply does not fit the available facts—scripturally or scientifically. Furthermore, the Scriptures speak to the fact that God existed prior to, and apart from, that which He created. As he began the book of Revelation, the apostle John described God as "the Alpha and the Omega...who is and who was and who is to come" (1:8). The psalmist wrote: "Before the mountains were brought forth, or ever thou hadst formed the earth and the world, even from everlasting to everlasting, thou art God" (90:2).

Third, we need to expose the illogical and unscriptural position within pantheism which teaches that God is an "impersonal It" rather than a personal God. As Sauer remarked: "It is also *a priori* impossible to accept an **unconscious intelligence**. This is a contradiction in terms. Similarly it is impossible to speak of unconscious ideas, for ideas demand a conscious, rational principle which produces them" (1962, p. 157, emp. added). In commenting on the same problem, Geisler wrote:

> [G]ranting that there are no real finite selves or "I's," then there is no such thing as an I-Thou relationship between finite selves nor between man and God. Both fellowship and worship become impossible. All alleged I-Thou or I-I relations reduce to I.... Religious experience is impossible in any meaningful sense of the term since all meaningful experience involves something or someone other than oneself with whom one enters the changing experience (1976, pp. 187-189).

How, we must ask, is it possible to communicate (physically or spiritually) with an impersonal, unconscious "It"?

Fourth, pantheists believe that God is the one absolute, unchanging reality. Yet they also believe it is possible for humans to come to realize that they are God. But if humans come to realize something, then they have changed along the way. A process has occurred that brought them from a point where they **did not know** they were God to a point where they **now know they are God**. That is to say, a "change" has occurred. As Geisler and Brooks put it: "But God cannot change. Therefore, anyone who 'comes to realize that he is God' isn't! The unchanging God always knew that He is God" (1990, p. 46). The pantheist cannot have it both ways.

Fifth, the concept of self-deification inherent in pantheism (e.g., MacLaine's sandy beach proclamation, "I am God!") must be opposed. It is here that the conflict between pantheism and Christianity is most obvious. Through the prophet Ezekiel, God told the king of Tyre: "Thou hast said, 'I am a god, I sit in the seat of God, in the midst of the seas'; yet thou art man, and not God, though thou didst set thy heart as the heart of God" (Ezekiel 28:2). In the Bible, only the wicked elevate themselves to the status of deity. King Herod flirted with self-deification—and died in a horrific manner as a result. Luke reported the event in his gospel as follows:

> So on a set day Herod, arrayed in royal apparel, sat on his throne and gave an oration to them. And the people kept shouting, "The voice of a god and not the voice of a man!" Then immediately an angel of the Lord struck him, because he did not give glory to God. And he was eaten of worms and died (Acts 12:21-23).

This stands in stark contradistinction to the reaction of Paul and Barnabas when the heathens at Lystra attempted to worship them (Acts 14:8-18). Had they been pantheists, these two preachers would have encouraged the crowds in Lystra to recognize not only the preachers' deity but their own deity as well! Yet, consider the response they offered instead:

> They rent their garments, and sprang forth among the multitude, crying out and saying, "Sirs, why do ye these things? We also are men of like passions with you, and bring you good tidings, that ye should turn from these vain things unto a living God, who made the heaven and the earth and the sea, and all that in them is" (Acts 14:14-15).

The testimony of the creation is not that man is God, but rather that God transcends both this world and its inhabitants. In Romans 1, the apostle Paul spoke directly to this point.

> For the wrath of God is revealed from heaven against all ungodliness and unrighteousness of men, who hinder the truth in unrighteousness; because that which is known of God is manifest in them; for God manifested it unto them. For the invisible things of him since the creation of the world are clearly seen, being perceived through the things that are made, even his everlasting power and divinity; that they may be without excuse: because that, knowing God, they glorified him not as God, neither gave thanks; but became vain in their reasonings, and their senseless heart was darkened. Professing themselves to be wise, they became fools, and changed the glory of the incorruptible God for the likeness of an image of corruptible man, and of birds, and four-footed beasts, and creeping things. Wherefore God gave them up in the lusts of their hearts unto uncleanness, that their bodies should be dishonored among themselves: for that they exchanged the truth of God for a lie, and worshipped and served the creature rather than the Creator, who is blessed for ever (Romans 1:18-25).

The idea of self-deification that is so prevalent in pantheism effectively eliminates the entire scheme of redemption and negates 4,000 years of Heaven's interaction in men's lives. It denies the role of Jesus in creation (John 1:1-3), the amazing prophetic accuracy of the Old and New Testaments (1 Peter 1:10-12), the providential preservation of the messianic seed (Galatians 3:16), the miraculous birth of Christ (Isaiah 7:14; Matthew 1:21-23), the significance of His resurrection (1 Corinthians 15), and the hope of His second coming (1 Thessalonians 4:13-18). When man decides to declare his own deity, he foments rebellion against the legitimate Inhabitant of heaven's throne. And he will bear the consequences of that rebellion, just as angels of old did (Jude 6).

Sixth, and last, Christians need to help others see that pantheism is little more than "disguised atheism." As Sauer put it:

Moreover, pantheism is, logically considered, only a polite form of atheism. For if one asserts that God and the world are the same, finally this comes to the same thing as saying "There is only one world, but there is no God." 'The statement of pantheism, "God and the world are one," is only a polite way of sending the Lord God about His business' (Schopenhauer) [1962, p. 157].

Geisler noted:

...if God is "All" or coextensive in his being with the universe, then pantheism is metaphysically indistinguishable from atheism. Both hold in common that the Whole is a collection of all the finite parts or aspects. The only difference is that the pantheist decides to attribute religious significance to the All and the atheist does not. But philosophically the Whole is identical, namely, one eternal self-contained system of reality (1976, p. 190).

Like atheism, pantheism offers no moral absolutes. Since each person is "God," each person does what is right in his own eyes. As in atheism, situation ethics rules supreme. The utopian hope of a planet and its inhabitants "united" or "one" with God is a pipe dream. In the concluding chapter of their book, *Apologetics in the New Age: A Critique of Pantheism*, Clark and Geisler succinctly wrote of what they called the "false hope" of pantheism, and then went on to say: "It lacks substance. The evidence that such a transformation will take place is sadly lacking. **Hope without realism is cruel**" (1990, p. 235, emp. added).

Pantheism is cruel indeed. In the truest tradition of Satan's temptation of Eve in the Garden of Eden, it convinces man to set himself up as God. The results then were tragic for the entire human race. The results of accepting pantheism in our day and age will prove to be no less so.

Panentheism

Although the names may sound somewhat familiar, pantheism and pan**en**theism actually are quite different. Whereas pantheism teaches that God **is** the world, panentheism teaches that

God is **in** the world. In panentheism, God is neither beyond the world nor identical with it. Rather, the world is God's body. "Further, unlike the God of theism, the panentheistic god does not create the world out of nothing (*ex nihilo*) but out of his own eternal sources (*ex Deo*)" [Geisler, 1997, p. 19].

Kreeft and Tacelli, in their *Handbook of Christian Apologetics*, have suggested that panentheism is

> ...a kind of compromise between theism and pantheism. It does not identify God with the material universe (as pantheism does), but neither does it hold that there actually exists an eternal God, transcendent to creation (as theism does). Panentheists believe that the material universe constitutes God, but that God is more than the material universe.... Thus panentheism is one way of making God temporal (1994, p. 94).

Another way of expressing God's temporal nature is to say that He is "finite" (as opposed to infinite). In fact, panentheism often is referred to by the synonym, "finite Godism." Another phrase used to describe panentheism is "process theology"—a concept that needs to be explained here.

The idea of "process theology" as expressed in its current form essentially is the brainchild of philosopher Alfred North Whitehead who penned several influential books on the subject, including *Process and Reality* (1929), *Adventures of Ideas* (1933), and *Modes of Thought* (1938). For those of us who are non-philosophers (or not even very philosophically oriented), process theology can seem a little like wading into a gently flowing creek that unexpectedly turns into a raging torrent. The first few steps do not begin to prepare you for what is yet to follow. Allow me to explain.

According to Whitehead (and other eminent proponents of process theology like Samuel Alexander, Charles Hartshorne, and Schubert Ogden), God is composed of two "poles" (thus, He is "bipolar," which is why another synonym for panentheism is "bipolar theism"). First, there is what is known as His **primor-**

dial pole, which is eternal, unchanging, ideal, and beyond the world. Second, however, there is what is known as His **consequent** pole, which is temporal, changing, real, and identical to the world. The primordial nature of God is His "potential" pole— i.e., what He **can be**. The consequent nature is his "actual" pole— i.e., what He **actually is** at any given moment. Geisler and Brooks have explained this as follows:

> So the world is not different from God; it is one of God's poles. His potential pole inhabits the world just like a soul inhabits a body. There it becomes actualized or real. So what the world is, is what God has become. As such God is never actually perfect; He is only striving toward perfection.... So God is always changing as the world changes. He in the **process** of becoming all that He can be (1989, pp. 48,47, emp. in orig.).

Since God is in the "process" of becoming all that He can be (sounds like the U.S. Army recruitment campaign slogan, doesn't it?), the concept is known as "process theology." And if you are wondering right about now if this is just a tad convoluted and thus a bit difficult to follow, let me set your mind at ease. Yes, it is! Therefore, in order to help explain what all of this means in "plain English," I would like to provide the following well-written, simplified summary from Winfried Corduan's book, *Reasonable Faith*.

> To understand the nature of God in Whitehead's system, we must come to terms with how Whitehead wants us to think of the world.... Put briefly, rather than thinking of things that change, we ought to think of **changes that take on the forms of things**. Take the following example. Let us say we are watching a football game. We see players, referees, cheerleaders, and spectators. They are running, kicking whistling, clapping, and shouting. Whitehead would want us to reverse the picture and think of the actions first with the people second. We observe running, kicking, whistling, clapping, and shouting which has taken on the form of players, referees, cheerleaders, and spectators. The action is of first order. In fact, it would be correct to say that we are observing "the football game event."

This is strange language intended to make the point that nothing is as fundamental to the world as change. White-head even wanted us to think of the whole universe as one big event.

What is change? Suppose we bake a cake. We mix to-gether the ingredients and create a batter. Then we put the batter into the oven and out comes a cake. We changed the batter into a cake. The batter had the potential to become a cake, but it was only after the change took place that it ac-tually was a cake. The potential cake became the actual cake; in other words, the potential of the batter to become a cake was actualized. All change can be understood in this way. When something changes, a potential has been actu-alized.

So when Whitehead says that the world is one big event, we need to picture it in terms of constant change. Thus the world must consist of two parts—or poles—an actual pole and a potential pole. The actual pole is everything that is true of the world at a given moment. The potential pole is the vast reservoir of everything that the world is not but can **become**. As the world is changing, potential is constantly being actualized. Picture an arrow in perpetual motion flow-ing from the potential to the actual side.

In this picture created by Whitehead, God watches over this process. Keep in mind that this God is supposed to be finite; He too changes. We must think of God in the same terms as the world: He has a potential pole and an actual pole (though Whitehead calls them God's "primordial" and "consequent" natures). Every moment some new potential in God is actualized; He changes in response to changes in the world.

Like the God of deism, the process God does not intervene in the world. He is strictly finite. In the football game of real-ity, He is the cheerleader. He presents the world with ideals to aim for; He entices the world to follow His plans; He grieves if the world strays; but He cannot make the world do anything. As the world changes, He changes, too, in or-der to coax the world along. Whatever He wants done needs to be accomplished by the world apart from His di-rect help (1993, pp. 96-97, emp. in orig.).

According to its advocates, then, panentheism avoids the pitfalls of some its major counterparts while at the same time partaking of the beneficial essence of strict theism. For example, in deism God is supposed to be an infinite Creator, yet One that does not perform miracles. In panentheism, since God is finite and not seen as omnipotent, panentheists suggest that there would be no inconsistency between a supernatural (but finite) being and the denial of the possibility of miracles. In pantheism, God **is** the world. Not so in panentheism; The world merely is **in** Him (His potential is constantly being actualized/realized). But, like true theism, panentheism envisions a God Who is the Author of moral commandments, and Who gives mankind the freedom of will to obey or disobey.

What should be the response of Christians to panentheism? First, we should be quick to point out that a "finite" God is worthless. As Corduan lamented:

> Once we have denied that God is infinite, we do not have any reason to think that He should be any of those other wonderful things that we say He is. Then He lacks a rationale for His being all-knowing, all-loving, eternal, and the other attributes that are based on His infinity. Take away the infinity, and you take away the justification for believing any of the standard attributes of God. Thus the arbitrary denial of any one attribute does not yield a **finite** God but yields **nothing at all** (1993, p. 95, emp. added).

This is an extremely important point. Once God's infinity is removed, most of His other traits fall one by one like the proverbial row of dominoes. A finite God, for example, cannot be an omniscient God. Consider the following. Panentheists place great faith in modern physics. In fact, much of Whitehead's "process theology" was based on concepts from physics. But according to the laws of physics, nothing travels faster than the speed of light (186,317 miles per second). That being true, then God never would be able to comprehend the entire Universe at once because

...his mind could not travel across the universe any father than 186,000+ miles per second. But by the time he has moved from one end of the universe to the other, the universe would have changed multimillions upon trillions of times. In this case, God would not really know the universe (his "body") at all. He could only know an infinitesimal portion at a time while all else is changing.... Of course, panentheists could solve their problem by affirming that God's mind transcends the universe and is not subject to the speed of light. But if they take this way out of the dilemma, they fall right into the arms of classical theism, which they strongly reject. So the painful alternative for panentheism is to retain an incoherent view or else return to theism (Geisler, 1997, p. 67).

Dr. Geisler is absolutely correct in this particular criticism of panentheism. One writer assessed the situation as follows:

The incontestable fact is that if God moves necessarily in time he is limited to some rate of velocity that is finite (say, the speed of light, if not the faster rate of some hypothetical tachyon). This means, unfortunately for process theism, that it is impossible for such a finite deity to have a simultaneous God's-eye view of the whole universe at once, since it would take him millions of light years or more to receive requisite data from distant points and places (Gruenler, 1983, p. 58, parenthetical comment in orig).

Thus, panentheism finds itself in the untenable status of positing a finite, non-omnipotent, non-omniscient God Who is best described in the following illogical manner. (1) He has the entire Universe as His body. (b) By definition, however, He is limited (because He is finite) by the physical laws of that Universe. (c) Therefore, He cannot even know His own body because it extends over the entire Universe, yet He cannot extend Himself over the entire Universe because He is restrained by its physical laws. Corduan could not have been more correct when he wrote: "Thus the arbitrary denial of any one attribute does not yield a **finite** God but yields **nothing at all**."

Second, panentheism suggests that God is in the "process" of changing, yet the crucial element of change—causality—is conspicuously missing. While it is correct to say that every change is the actualization of some potential, such change does not occur by itself. There must be a **cause** involved in the process. Remember the cake analogy above?

> Try actualizing a bowl of batter's potential to become a cake without putting it into an oven. A coffee cup has the potential to be filled with coffee, so let us see if it will fill itself. Of course it won't. Cakes cannot bake themselves; coffee cups cannot fill themselves; **potentials cannot actualize themselves**. Where a change occurs, there must be a cause to bring about that change.... Panentheism attempts to circumvent the principle of causality. In its picture of God and the world there is constant change. Potentials are actualized, but the cause is missing. This is a particularly embarrassing deficiency when it comes to its understanding of God.... Either his or her God is the metaphysical impossibility of a potential that actualizes itself (akin to the coffee cup which fills itself) or there has to be a cause outside of God (a God behind God) that actualizes His potential. This would mean that God is no longer in any recognizable sense. Either an impossible God or a God who is not really God; this is the panentheist's dilemma. It boils down to practical atheism (Corduan, 1993, pp. 97,98, emp. and parenthetical comments in orig.).

In other words, panentheism needs theism's God in order to "actualize" its God—which turns out after all not to be God but instead some sort of giant "creature" that needs a more ultimate and real cause than itself. The entire panentheistic scenario becomes the old "which came first, the chicken or the egg" routine. If the potential pole came before the actual, how, then, was anything actualized? Yet the actual pole certainly could not have come first, because it had no potential to become. As Geisler and Brooks have pointed out, when it comes to "potential" poles and "actual" poles

[p]anentheists would say that they always existed together, but then we have to face the fact that time cannot go back into the past forever. The only answer can be that something else created the whole ball of wax. It took a creator beyond the process.... It took a transcendent God to create a chicken who would lay eggs (1990, pp. 50,51).

Third, panentheism is the grand example of man creating God in **his** image, rather than the reverse (which no doubt is why Norman Geisler titled his book critiquing panentheism, *Creating God in the Image of Man?*). Panentheists make the mistake of confusing God's unchanging **attributes** with His changing **activities**. And once that fatal error has been committed, God then is viewed as what He **does** rather than what He **is**. As Geisler has warned, with such a system

[t]here is activity but no Actor, movement but no Mover, creation but no Creator. Beginning with an anthropomorphic bipolar model of God, it is no wonder that the god of panentheism emerges finite, limited in knowledge, goodness, and power, and in possession of a physical body like the rest of us. Whatever else may be said of this whittling of God down to man's level and form, it is surely not the God presented in the Bible (1976, p. 210).

The God of panentheism most certainly is not the God of the Bible. Do the Scriptures speak of God engaging in temporal, changing **actions** on occasion? Certainly. In fact, the Bible uses a number of different metaphors drawn from specific human analogies. For example, God is said to "repent" (Jonah 3:10), to have "arms" (Psalm 136:12), to see with "eyes" (Hebrews 4:13), and to hear with His "ear" (Isaiah 59:1-2). Yet the Bible also speaks of God as a "rock" (Psalm 18:2), a "tower" (Proverbs 18:10), and as having "wings" (Psalm 91:4). If one wishes to use these metaphors to frame a personal concept of God (as panentheists attempt to do), two things first must be acknowledged. (1) The Bible uses metaphorical/anthropomorphic terminology that is intended to assist humans (who are finite) as they grapple with the spiritual nature of God (Who is infinite). (2) At times, the images that are used are mutually conflicting (some speak of minerals [a rock], some speak of animal characteristics [wings], and some speak of human traits [arms, ears, eyes, etc.]. It is not a proper use of Scripture to take these images and apply them in a literal fashion to make the Universe God's body. Furthermore, such an attempt ignores additional passages of Scripture which teach that God, as a Spirit (John 4:24), is both infinite (Psalm 147:5) and unchanging (Malachi 3:6; Hebrews 6:18; James 1:17).

Panentheism has little to recommend it, and much to dissuade us from accepting it. The "god" of panentheism can "coax" us, but not command us. He can fight evil, but never triumph over it. He allegedly intends to achieve a better world with human cooperation, yet most of the world is happily oblivious to the His existence. He is supposed to be able to achieve a better world, but is limited by the physical laws of that world so that He never can achieve more than those laws will allow. As Norman Geisler put it:

> How can anyone worship a god so impotent that he cannot even call the whole thing off? Is not such a god so paralyzed as to be perilous?... [A]s a total world view, the God of panentheism does not fill the bill. The basic dipolar concept of God as eternal potential seeking temporal actualization is self-defeating. No potential can activate itself; and if there is some pure actuality outside the panentheistic God that actualizes it, then one must posit a theistic God of pure act in order to account for the panentheistic God.... By comparison a theistic God is more adequate both metaphysically and personally (1976, pp. 210,213).

3

CAUSES OF UNBELIEF

Most rational, reasonable people would agree that actions have consequences. If a man commits a crime, is pursued and apprehended by law enforcement officers, tried by a jury of his peers, and sentenced to life in the penitentiary or death in the electric chair, who is responsible? When an individual decides to act, is it not true that ultimately the consequences of those actions fall squarely on his or her shoulders? Indeed, actions **do** have consequences.

But so do beliefs and ideas. Is that not one reason why the spoken word is so powerful. The ability to elucidate an idea via a speech, lecture, or other oral presentation can produce astonishing consequences. Think, for example, of the late president of the United States, John F. Kennedy, who inspired Americans with his "Ask not what your country can do for you, but what you can do for your country" inaugural speech. On the heels of his idea—presented so eloquently by a dashing, young, newly elected, and extremely popular president—volunteerism in American grew at an unprecedented rate. Or, reflect upon another presentation in our nation's capital by the late, slain civil rights leader, Martin Luther King, Jr. The moving oratory in his "I have a dream" speech captured the attention of an entire nation, and culminated in legislation aimed at protecting the rights of **all** citizens, regardless of their ethnic background, skin color, or religious beliefs.

Beliefs and ideas presented via the written word are no less powerful. Ponder such documents as the hallowed United States *Constitution* that serves as the basis for the freedoms every citizen enjoys. Or contemplate the beloved *Declaration of Independence* that guarantees every American certain "unalienable rights." Throughout the history of mankind, the written word has expressed ideas that manifested the ability to free men and women (e.g., the English *Magna Carta*) or to enslave them (e.g., Adolf Hitler's *Mein Kampf*).

Indeed, beliefs and ideas—like actions—have consequences. Prominent humanist Martin Gardner devoted an entire chapter in one of his books to "The Relevance of Belief Systems," in an attempt to explain that **what a person believes** profoundly influences **how a person acts** (1988, pp. 57-64). In his book, *Does It Matter What I Believe?*, Millard J. Erickson, wrote that there are numerous reasons

> ...why having correct beliefs is important. Our whole lives are inevitably affected by the real world around us, so what we believe about it is of the utmost importance.... What we believe about reality does not change the truth, nor its effect upon us. Correct belief, however, enables us to know the truth as it is, and then to take appropriate action, so that it will have the best possible effect upon our lives. Having correct beliefs is also necessary because of the large amount and variety of incorrect beliefs which are about (1992, pp. 12,13).

Consider then, in this context, belief in the existence of God. Surely it is safe to say that practically no single belief in the thousands of years of recorded human history has produced as many, or as varied a set of, consequences as this one idea. It has been studied and debated from time immemorial. It has been responsible for some of the most impassioned speeches of which the human spirit is capable. It has engendered multiplied millions of pages of text upon which billions of words—both pro and con—have been written. And, ultimately, it has produced as a consequence either belief or unbelief—both of which have serious implications. Erickson was correct when he suggested that "having correct beliefs is important." In the past, I have examined reasons for **belief** in the God of the Bible (e.g., Thompson, 1995a, 1995b; Thompson and Jackson, 1982, 1996). I now would like to examine causes of **unbelief**.

Bias Against God

There is little doubt that in many instances of unbelief non-rational factors are a primary influence. H.H. Farmer put it like this: "There can be no question that many people find belief in God difficult because there is in their mind a bias which predisposes them against it" (1942, p. 129). This built-in bias is what Stanley Sayers has referred to as "the prejudice of unbelief." Writing under that title in his book, *Optimism in an Age of Peril*, he said: "One of the significant and obvious reasons the unbeliever remains an unbeliever is that **he likes it that way**. In fact, any evidence of any source or to any degree fails to move him from his position if his heart is strongly bent **against** evidence and **toward** unbelief" (1973, p. 43, emp. in orig.).

Consider the well-documented case of Charles Darwin. James Bales wrote concerning the now-famous popularizer of organic evolution: "For some reason or another, Darwin was determined not to believe in God. Although he admitted more than once that it is reasonable to believe in God, and unreasonable to reject God, yet so determined was he not to believe that he slew reason when reason led him to God" (1976, p. 17). Bales' assessment is correct, as is evident from Darwin's own comments. He wrote, for example:

This follows from the extreme difficulty or rather impossibility of conceiving this immense and wonderful universe, including man with his capacity for looking far backwards and far into futurity, as the result of blind chance or necessity. When thus reflecting I feel compelled to look to a First Cause having an intelligent mind in some degree analogous to that of man; and I deserve to be called a Theist. This conclusion was strong in my mind about the time, as far as I can remember, when I wrote the *Origin of Species*; and it is since that time that it has very gradually, with many fluctuations, become weaker. But then arises the doubt, can the mind of man, which has, as I fully believe, been developed from a mind as low as that possessed by the lowest animals, be trusted when it draws such grand conclusions? (as quoted in Francis Darwin, 1898, 1:282).

Apparently, a singular event in Darwin's life set him irreversibly on the road to unbelief. In 1850, Charles and Emma Darwin's oldest daughter, Annie, fell ill. On April 23, 1851, she died at the tender age of ten. Darwin was devastated. Although Emma was a devout believer in God and Christianity, with Annie's death her husband no longer could stomach such concepts. In their massive, scholarly biography, *Darwin*, Desmond and Moore wrote:

This was the end of the road, the crucifixion of his hopes. He could not believe the way Emma believed—nor **what** she believed. There was no straw to clutch, no promised resurrection. Christian faith was futile.... For him the death marked an impasse and a new beginning. It put an end to three years' deliberation about the Christian meaning of mortality; it opened up a fresh vision of the tragic contingency of nature.... Annie's cruel death destroyed Charles's tatters of belief in a moral, just universe. Later he would say that this period chimed the final death-knell for his Christianity, even if it had been a long, drawn-out process of decay.... Charles now took his stand as an unbeliever (1991, pp. 384,386,387, emp. in orig.).

In speaking of his now-abandoned belief in God, Darwin eventually admitted: "But I found it more and more difficult, with free scope given to my imagination, to invent evidence which would suffice to convince me. Thus disbelief crept over me at such a slow rate, but at last was complete. The rate was so slow that I felt no distress" (as quoted in Francis Darwin, 1898, 1:277-278; cf. also Greene, 1963, pp. 16-17). Bales therefore concluded:

> Darwin, so far as my research shows, never used doubt as to the reliability of human reason to discredit other positions. He did not say that since Darwinism was the product of his mind, therefore it could not be trusted. It was only when reason led him to God that he destroyed reason. What a strong bias against God he must have had. Is it not strange? Darwin said that the animal origin of man's mind keeps man from being fully able to trust his reasoning, and yet he said that **he fully believed** that man originated that way. Darwin should either have doubted all reasoning, including Darwinism, or have admitted that the human mind is not wholly an untrustworthy instrument. There are other things which could be said about these quotations from Darwin, but our purpose here is to show that he had a powerful bias against God.... [R]eason led him to God. So he got rid of reason (1976, pp. 17-18, emp. in orig.; cf. also R.E.D. Clark's, *Darwin: Before and After*, 1948, for other aspects of Darwin's flight from God).

Darwin's personal bias against God—brought to fruition when his ten-year-old daughter, Annie, died—ultimately allowed disbelief to root out belief. As Bales went on to observe, a person "cannot be coerced into accepting truth on any subject.... With reference to faith...as with reference to other things, man is still free to choose" (1976, pp. 94,95). Simply put, some people today carry within them a stubborn determination **not** to believe in God. It can have **little** to do with a lack of credible evidence and **much** to do with a built-in bias against belief in God in the first place. In the chapter, "Flight from an Indignant God," in his book *If There's a God, Why Are There Atheists?*, R.C. Sproul commented on this very point when he wrote:

> ...unbelief is generated not so much by intellectual causes as by moral and psychological ones.... Though people are not persuaded by the evidence, this does not indicate an insufficiency in the evidence, but rather an insufficiency in

man. **This insufficiency is not a natural inability that provides man with an excuse.** Man's failure to see this general and universal revelation of God is not because he lacks eyes or ears or a brain with which to think. The problem is not a lack of knowledge or a lack of natural cognitive equipment but a moral deficiency.... The problem is not that there is insufficient evidence to convince rational human beings that there is a God, but that rational human beings have a **natural hostility to the being of God**.... Man's desire is not that the omnipotent, personal Judeo-Christian God **exist**, but that He **not exist** (1978, pp. 57, 58, emp. added).

In Northampton, Massachusetts in 1976, the famed preacher Jonathan Edwards presented a sermon titled, "Men are Naturally God's Enemies," in which he gave a lengthy exposition of Romans 5:10—"For if when we were enemies...." The point of the lesson was that men, by their behavior, have documented in an incontrovertible manner their inner hostility toward God. Edwards said:

They are enemies in the natural relish of their souls. They have an inbred distaste and disrelish of God's perfections. God is not such a sort of being as they would have. Though they are ignorant of God, yet from what they hear of Him, and from what is manifest by the light of nature of God, they do not like Him. By His being endowed with such attributes as He is, they have an aversion to Him. They hear God is an infinitely holy, pure, and righteous Being, and they do not like Him upon this account; they have no relish of such kind of qualifications; they take no delight in contemplating them. It would be a mere task, a bondage to a natural man, to be obliged to set himself to contemplate these attributes of God. They see no manner of beauty or loveliness nor taste any sweetness in them. And upon the account of their distaste of these perfections, they dislike all the other of His attributes. They have greater aversion to Him because He is omniscient and knows all things; because His omniscience is a holy omniscience. They are not pleased that He is omnipotent, and can do whatever He pleases; because it is a holy omnipotence. They are enemies even to His mercy, because it is a holy mercy. They do not like His immutability, because by this He never will be otherwise than He is, an infinitely holy God (1879, 4:38).

In his book, *If There's a God, Why Are There Atheists?*, R.C. Sproul included a chapter called "The Never-Ending Bias," in which he wrote:

> The theme [of his book—BT] is that natural man suffers from prejudice. He operates within a framework of insufferable bias against the God of Christianity. The Christian God is utterly repugnant to him because He represents the threat of threats to man's own desires and ambitions. The will of man is on a collision course with the will of God. Such a course leads inevitably to a conflict of interests.... Men would apparently rather die in their sin than live forever in obedience (1978, p. 146).

Paul reminded the Christians in Rome of those who, "knowing God, glorified him not as God, neither gave thanks; but became vain in their reasonings, and their senseless heart was darkened. And even as they refused to have God in their knowledge, God gave them up unto a reprobate mind" (Romans 1:21,28). The problem about which the apostle wrote was not a failure to accept what was **unknowable** (the text in Romans clearly indicates that these were people who could, and did, know of the existence of God). Rather, it was a problem of refusing to accept what was **knowable**—i.e., God's reality.

Those to whom Paul referred had such a built-in prejudice against God (what Sproul labeled "the never-ending bias") that they abjectly **refused** to have God in their knowledge. This situation, then, caused the apostle to write (by inspiration of the Holy Spirit) that "professing themselves to be wise, they became fools" (Romans 1:22).

In biblical usage, the term "fool" generally does not indicate a person of diminished intelligence, and it certainly is not used here in such a fashion. Instead, the term carries both a moral and religious judgment. As Bertram has noted:

> With reference to men the use is predominantly psychological. The word implies censure on man himself: his acts, thoughts, counsels, and words are not as they should be.

The weakness may be due to a specific failure in judgment or decision, but a general deficiency of intellectual and spiritual capacities may also be asserted (1971, 4:832).

This is why the psalmist (again, writing by inspiration) said that "the fool hath said in his heart, there is no God" (14:1). If "the fear of the Lord is the beginning of wisdom" (Psalm 111:10), then, conversely, foolishness finds its origin in the rejection of God. Isaiah referred to a man as a fool whose "mind plots iniquity to practice ungodliness" and whose attitude of practical atheism causes him to "utter error concerning the Lord" (Isaiah 32:5, RSV). When Paul wrote his first epistle to the Christians in Corinth, he observed that "the natural man receiveth not the things of the Spirit of God: for they are foolishness unto him" (1 Corinthians 2:14). Bias against God thus has become one of the chief causes of unbelief, which no doubt explains why the Hebrew writer warned: "Take heed, brethren, lest haply there shall be in any one of you an **evil heart of unbelief** in falling away from the living God" (Hebrews 3:12).

Parents and Upbringing

In Romans 14:7, Paul stated that "none of us liveth to himself, and none dieth to himself." The essence of that thought has been perpetuated in the saying that "no man is an island." How true an observation that is. From the beginning to the end of this pilgrimage we call "life," we interact socially with those around us. But surely one of the most formidable influences upon any human being comes in the form of parents. Generally speaking, mothers and fathers have not only an initial, but a continuing effect upon their offspring. Children are born with sponge-like minds that begin basically as "blank slates" upon which parents have a grand opportunity (and awesome responsibility!) to write. It has been said that a child's mind is like Jell-O® and that the parents' task is to put in all the "good stuff" before it "sets."

Sometimes that task is accomplished by instruction, which is why parents are admonished to teach and nurture their children "in the chastening and admonition of the Lord" (Ephesians 6:4). Sometimes it is accomplished by discipline, which is why the Proverbs writer wisely observed that "the rod and reproof give wisdom; but a child left to himself causeth shame to his mother" (29: 15). And sometimes it is accomplished by exemplary behavior that provides a proper example, which is why the apostle Peter discussed those very things in the context of a family relationship. He spoke of the potential effect a godly wife could have upon her unbelieving husband when he wrote: "In like manner, ye wives be in subjection to your own husbands; that, even if any obey not the word, they may without a word be gained by the behavior of their wives, beholding your chaste behavior coupled with fear" (1 Peter 3:1-2). What a sobering thought—that one person (e.g., a godly wife), through consistently impressive behavior tempered by a reverent fear of God, could set such a good example that another person (e.g., an unbelieving husband) might be convicted of God's existence and convinced to obey His will.

But consider the obvious corollary to this principle. If accurate instruction, timely discipline, and a proper example coupled with faithfulness can produce such wonderful results, what results might inaccurate instruction, a lack of discipline, and an improper example coupled with unfaithfulness produce? Does not practical experience answer that question in a thousand different ways? Although at times we wish they did not, the truth of the matter is that more often than not the decisions we make, and the actions that stem from those decisions, inevitably affect those we love the most. Certainly this is true in a spiritual context. One expert in child psychology put it this way:

> I believe that much atheism has the ground prepared for it in the disillusionment with the parent which has arisen in the child. Disbelief in life, skepticism about humanity, the denial of God—all sink their roots in the soil of emotion

long before exposure to courses in philosophy and science. Life has scarred such people early and has made them unwilling to believe either in man or in God (Liebman, 1946, pp. 147-148).

Is it not the case that children often are influenced—rightly or wrongly—by the attitudes and actions of their parents? As proof of this point, consider the following real-life situation. One of the foremost unbelievers of our day is Harvard's famed paleontologist, Stephen Jay Gould. Dr. Gould—an indefatigable crusader on behalf of organic evolution—is a cogent writer and a gifted speaker, as well as one of the evolutionary establishment's most prolific and best-read authors. The January 1983 issue of *Discover* magazine designated him "Scientist of the Year," he often was featured as a special guest on Phil Donahue's television talk show, and through the past two or three decades his articles have appeared frequently not only in refereed scientific journals (e.g., *Science*, *New Scientist*, *Paleobiology*, etc.), but in popular science magazines as well (*Discover*, *Omni*, *Science Digest*, and others). In addition, he is the co-developer (with Niles Eldredge from the American Museum of Natural History) of the popular concept known as "punctuated equilibrium" that provides a new twist regarding the tempo and mode of evolution. All this being true, when Dr. Gould speaks, many people listen. Gould himself has suggested: "When we come to popular writing about evolution, I suppose that my own essays are as well read as any" (1987, 8[1]:67). One writer described him in these words:

> ...Stephen Jay Gould is as charming on television and in his popular essays about his atheism as he is about his love of baseball. Gould is almost jolly in his condescending remarks about religionists, patting such minor minds on the head with avuncular goodwill, as one might humor a foolish relative (Lockerbie, 1998, p. 229).

Interestingly, relatives and atheism share a common connection in Gould's life. In his 1999 book, *Rocks of Ages: Science and Religion in the Fullness of Life*, Dr. Gould discussed his early years

...in a New York Jewish family following the standard pattern of generational rise: immigrant grandparents who started in the sweatshops, parents who reached the lower ranks of the middle classes but had no advanced schooling, and my third generation, headed for a college education and a professional life to fulfill the postponed destiny (p. 7).

His "New York Jewish family," however, was different than most, as he explained.

I shared the enormous benefits of a respect for learning that pervades Jewish culture, even at the poorest economic levels. But **I had no formal religious education** —I did not even have a bar mitzvah—**because my parents had rebelled** against a previously unquestioned family background. (In my current judgment, they rebelled too far, but opinions on such questions tend to swing on a pendulum from one generation to the next, perhaps eventually coming to rest at a wise center.) But my parents retained pride in Jewish history and heritage, **while abandoning all theology and religious belief**.... I am not a believer (1999a, p. 8, emp. added, parenthetical comments in orig.).

While many no doubt are aware of the fact that Dr. Gould is **not** "a believer," they may not be aware of the fact that he **is** a devout Marxist. Exactly where did Gould develop his Marxism, and the atheism that inevitably accompanies it? Through one of his parents! As Gould himself admitted: "It may also not be irrelevant to our personal preferences that one of us learned his Marxism, literally, at his daddy's knee" (Gould and Eldredge, 1977, 3: 145). In an article on "The Darwin Debate" in *Marxism Today*, Robert M. Young wrote that

Aspects of evolutionism are perfectly consistent with Marxism. The explanation of the origins of humankind and of mind by purely natural forces was, and remains, as welcome to Marxists as to any other secularists. The sources of value and responsibility are not to be found in a separate mental realm or in an immortal soul, much less in the inspired words of the Bible (1982, 26:21).

Indeed, it may "not be irrelevant" that as a youngster Stephen Jay Gould was reared in a family who "abandoned all theology and religious belief," enthusiastically embraced Marxism in their place, and subsequently immersed him in the godless, dialectical materialism of that doctrine—thereby producing one of the foremost evolutionists of our generation.

If children witness callous indifference, skepticism, or outright infidelity on the part of their parents in regard to spiritual matters, more often than not those children will exhibit the same callousness, skepticism, or infidelity in their own lives. And is it not also extremely likely that **their** children will be reared in the same atmosphere? (Ask yourself—what do you think Dr. Gould's own son is being taught by his father, and likely will grow up believing?) Thus, in the end, the spiritual condition of not one, but several generations has been affected adversely as a direct result of the instruction/example of parents and the subsequent upbringing received at their hands.

Education

Surely one of the most important causes of unbelief in the world today relates to the kind of education a person receives. [Please notice that I did **not** say unbelief "relates to the education" a person receives; rather, I said unbelief "relates to the **kind** of education" a person receives. I do not mean to "throw the baby out with the bath water" by suggesting that **all** education results in unbelief, for that most certainly is not the case and is not representative of my position.] Generally speaking, the educational system in America is the end product of John Dewey's "progressive education movement." The renowned humanistic philosopher, Will Durant, wrote that "there is hardly a school in America that has not felt his influence" (1961, p. 390). But it was not just American schools that Dewey influenced. In his book, *The Long War Against God*, Henry Morris discussed how the progressive education movement "profoundly changed education not only in America but also in many other countries" as well (1989, p. 38).

Dewey, who was a socialist and materialistic pantheist, was one of the founders (and the first president) of the American Humanist Association, formed in 1933. I have discussed Dewey's atheistic views elsewhere (see Thompson, 1994, 1999). At this juncture, I simply would like to make the point that as a result of Dewey's efforts through the educational establishment, the **kind** of education now being offered in many public schools has the potential to discourage or destroy faith in God, while at the same time encouraging and promoting unbelief. One of the most important tools employed by Dewey and his intellectual offspring to cripple belief was, and is, organic evolution. As Samuel Blumenfeld stated in his classic text, *NEA: Trojan Horse in American Education*:

> An absolute faith in science became the driving force behind the progressives.... The most important idea that would influence the educators was that of evolution—the notion that man, through a process of natural selection, had evolved to his present state from a common animal ancestry. Evolution was as sharp a break with the Biblical view of creation as anyone could make, and it was quickly picked up by those anxious to disprove the validity of orthodox religion (1984, p. 43).

Morris correctly assessed the post-Dewey situation when he wrote:

> The underlying assumption of progressive education was that the child is simply an evolved animal and must be trained as such—not as an individual created in God's image with tremendous potential as an individual. A child was considered but one member in a group and therefore must be trained collectively to fit into his or her appropriate place in society (1989, p. 48).

The child's "appropriate place in society"—specifically the humanistic society that Dewey and his cohorts envisioned—neither included nor allowed for belief in the God of the Bible. Thus, every effort was made to use the educational system to gain new recruits. Alfred Rehwinkel discussed just such a situation.

The shock received by the inexperienced young student is therefore overwhelming when he enters the classroom of such teachers and suddenly discovers to his great bewilderment that these men and women of acclaimed learning do not believe the views taught him in his early childhood days; and since the student sits at their feet day after day, it usually does not require a great deal of time until the foundation of his faith begins to crumble as stone upon stone is being removed from it by these unbelieving teachers. Only too often the results are disastrous. The young Christian becomes disturbed, confused, and bewildered. Social pressure and the weight of authority add to his difficulties. First he begins to doubt the infallibility of the Bible in matters of geology, but he will not stop there. Other difficulties arise, and before long skepticism and unbelief have taken the place of his childhood faith, and the saddest of all tragedies has happened. Once more a pious Christian youth has gained a glittering world of pseudo-learning but has lost his own immortal soul (1951, p. xvii).

Such a scenario is not merely theoretical, but practical. Consider as one example the case of renowned Harvard evolutionist, Edward O. Wilson, who is recognized worldwide as the "father of sociobiology." Wilson summarized his own youthful educational experience as follows:

As were many persons in Alabama, I was a born-again Christian. When I was fifteen, I entered the Southern Baptist Church with great fervor and interest in the fundamentalist religion. I left at seventeen when I got to the University of Alabama and heard about evolutionary theory (1982, p. 40).

Chet Raymo serves as yet another example of a person who once cherished his belief in God, but who ultimately lost his faith as a result of the kind of education he received. Raymo is a professor of physics and astronomy at Stonehill College in Massachusetts, has written a weekly column on science for the *Boston Globe* for more than a dozen years and was reared as a Roman Catholic. In his book, *Skeptics and True Believers*, he wrote:

I learned something else in my study of science, something that had an even greater effect upon my religious faith. None of the miracles I had been offered in my religious training were as impressively revealing of God's power as the facts that I was learning in science (1998, p. 20).

Little wonder, then, that the thesis of Raymo's book is that there is an unavoidable dichotomy between educated people of science who empirically "know" things and those in religion who spiritually "believe" things—with the educated, scientifically oriented folks obviously being on the more desirable end of the spectrum (and winning out in the end).

There can be little doubt that many today believe in evolution because it is what they have been taught. For the past century, evolution has been in the limelight. And for the past quarter of a century or more, it has been taught as **scientific fact** in many elementary, junior high, and senior high schools, as well as in most colleges and universities. Marshall and Sandra Hall have offered this summary.

> In the first place, evolution is what is taught in the schools. At least two, and in some cases three and four generations, have used textbooks that presented it as proven fact. The teachers, who for the most part learned it as truth, pass it on as truth. Students are as thoroughly and surely indoctrinated with the concept of evolution as students have ever been indoctrinated with any unproven belief (1974, p. 10).

In their book, *Why Scientists Accept Evolution*, Bales and Clark confirmed such an observation.

> Evolution is taken for granted today and thus it is uncritically accepted by scientists as well as laymen. It is accepted by them today because it was already accepted by others who went before them and under whose direction they obtained their education (1966, p. 106).

Further exacerbating the problem is the fact that evolution has been given the "stamp of approval" by important spokespersons from practically every field of human endeavor. While there have been those from politics, the humanities, the arts, and other fields who openly have defended evolution as factual, in no other area has this defense been as pronounced as in the sciences. Because science has seen so many successes, and because these successes have been so visible and well publicized, scientists have been granted an aura of respectability that only can be envied by non-scientists.

As a result, when scientists champion a cause, people generally take notice. After all, it is their workings through the scientific method that have eradicated smallpox, put men on the Moon, prevented polio, and lengthened human life spans. We have grown used to seeing "experts" from various scientific disciplines ply their trade in an endless stream of amazing feats. Heart surgery has become commonplace; organ transplants have become routine; space shuttles flying into the heavens have become standard fare.

Thus, when the atheistic concept of organic evolution is presented as something that "all reputable scientists believe," there are many people who accept such an assessment at face value, and who therefore fall in line with what they believe is a well-proven dictum that has been enshrouded with the cloak of scientific respectability. As atheistic philosopher Paul Ricci has written: "The reliability of evolution not only as a theory but as a principle of understanding is not contested by the vast majority of biologists, geologists, astronomers, and other scientists" (1986, p. 172). Or, as Stephen Jay Gould put it: "The fact of evolution is as well established as anything in science (as secure as the revolution of the earth around the sun), though absolute certainty has no place in our [scientists'—BT] lexicon (1987, 8[1]:64; parenthetical comment in orig). [In a guest editorial in the August 23, 1999 issue of *Time* magazine, Dr. Gould reiterated this point when he said that "...evolution is as well documented as any phenomenon in science, as strongly as the earth's revolution around the sun rather than vice versa. In this sense, we can call evolution a 'fact'" (1999b, p. 59).]

Such comments are intended to leave the impression that well-informed, intelligent people dare not doubt the truthfulness of organic evolution. The message is: "All scientists believe it; so should you." As Marshall and Sandra Hall inquired: "How, then, are people with little or no special knowledge of the various sciences and related subjects to challenge the authorities? It is natural to accept what 'experts' say, and most people do" (1974, p. 10). Henry Morris observed: "...the main reason most educated people believe in evolution is simply because they have been told that most educated people believe in evolution" (1963, p. 26).

Huston Smith, a leading philosopher and professor of religion at Syracuse University has commented on this phenomenon as follows:

> One reason education undoes belief is its teaching of evolution; Darwin's own drift from orthodoxy to agnosticism was symptomatic. Martin Lings is probably right in saying that "more cases of loss of religious faith are to be traced to the theory of evolution...than to anything else" (1982, p. 755; Lings' quote is from *Studies in Comparative Religion*, 1970, Winter).

Sir Julian Huxley, the famous UNESCO [United Nations Educational and Scientific Organization] biologist, put it this way: "Darwinism removed the whole idea of God as the creator of organisms from the sphere of rational discussion" (1960, p. 45).

The simple fact is, however, that truth is not determined by popular opinion or majority vote. A thing may be, and often is, true even when accepted only by the minority. Furthermore, a thing may be, and often is, false even though accepted by the majority. Believing something based on the assumption that "everyone else" also believes it often can lead to disastrous results. As Guy N. Woods remarked: "It is dangerous to follow the multitude because the majority is almost always on the wrong side in this world" (1982, 124[1]:2). Or, as Moses warned the children of Israel: "Thou shalt not follow a multitude to do evil" (Exodus 23:2).

Pride

When the Lord asked in John 5:44, "How can ye believe, who receive glory one of another, and the glory that cometh from the only God ye seek not?," He summed up one of the main reasons why many are unprepared to believe in God. Man is so busy seeking and reveling in his own glory that he has neither the time nor the inclination to offer glory to His Maker. An unhealthy lust for power wrapped in a cloak of pride breeds unbelief. German philosopher Friedrich Nietzsche (he of "God is dead" fame) expressed such an attitude when he asked a friend, "If there were gods, how could I endure it to be no god?" In his famous composition, *Invictus*, infidel poet William Ernest Henley wrote: "I am the master of my fate; I am the captain of my soul." The famed Harvard evolutionist, George Gaylord Simpson, ended one of his books with these words: "Man is his own master. He can and must decide and manage his own destiny" (1953, p. 155).

One of the most famous apologists among Christian theists of the past generation was the renowned biblical scholar Wilbur M. Smith. In 1945 he authored *Therefore Stand*, which was then, and is now, a classic in the field of Christian apologetics. In chapter three, under the heading of "Some Reasons for the Unbelief of Men and Their Antagonism Against God," Dr. Smith listed numerous causes of unbelief, one of which was "The Pride of Man." Included in his discussion of that subject was this observation:

> When man says he believes in a Supreme Being...he at the same time, if he is honest, confesses that God is holy, and he himself, unholy, that God is independent and can do according to His own will, while man is dependent. All this is humiliating; it takes away any cause for pride, for if there is one thing that man has always liked to feel it is that he is sufficient for all things, that he is going to bring about a better world by his own ingenuity, that he is the greatest and highest and most important phenomenon in the world, and that beyond him there is nothing worth considering (1974 reprint, p. 151).

In the text they co-authored, *A Survey of European Civilization: 1500-Present,* historians Walter Ferguson and Geoffrey Bruun discussed the "intellectual revolution" that had engulfed mankind. The following statement represents their assessment of the effects of this phenomenon: "The new learning offered man a more vain-glorious picture of himself, and rooted itself in his pride; whereas his religious beliefs had been the fruit of his humility" (1937, pp. 9-11). Forty years later, the accuracy of their assessment became clear when two eminent atheists of our generation, Richard Leakey and Roger Lewin, wrote:

> Unquestionably mankind **is** special, and in many ways, too.... There is now a critical need for a deep awareness that, no matter how special we are as an animal, we are still part of the greater balance of nature.... During that relatively brief span evolutionary pressures forged a brain capable of profound understanding of matters animate and inanimate: the fruits of intellectual and technological endeavour in this latter quarter of the 20th century give us just an inkling of what the human mind can achieve. The potential is enormous, almost infinite. **We can, if we so choose, do virtually anything**... (1977, p. 256; first emp. in orig., latter emp. added).

Smith's conclusion on "the pride of man" was: "As pride increases, humility decreases, and as man finds himself self-sufficient he will discard his religious convictions, or having none, he will fight those of others" (1974, pp. 152-153).

In America, one of Nietzsche's intellectual offspring was Thomas J.J. Altizer, a professor at Emory University in Atlanta, Georgia. Through two popular books, *Oriental Mysticism and Biblical Eschatology* (1961) and *The Gospel of Christian Atheism* (1966), he affirmed—like his German counterpart—that "God is dead." His position was not exactly the same as Nietzsche's, however. Altizer had concluded that the God of traditional theism was "dead." A transcendent God was a useless, mythical, powerless figurehead Who had no authority over mankind. Almost forty years earlier, Walter Lippmann had addressed this same type of problem in his book, *A Preface to Morals.*

This is the first age, I think, in the history of mankind when the circumstances of life have conspired with the intellectual habits of the time to render any fixed and authoritative belief incredible to large masses of men. The irreligion of the modern world is radical to a degree for which there is, I think, no counterpart.... I do not mean that modern men have ceased to believe in God. I do not mean that they no longer believe in Him simply and literally. I mean they have defined and refined their ideas of Him until they can no longer honestly say He exists... (1929, pp. 12,21).

In the mid-1960s, when Altizer's positions were receiving considerable publicity, James D. Bales authored an important and timely volume, *The God-Killer?* (1967), in which he reviewed and refuted Altizer's teachings. Almost a decade later, he still was exposing and opposing Altizer's views. In his book, *How Can Ye Believe?*, Dr. Bales wrote:

Although some have been brought up in confusion, and have not had time to do much thinking, the ultimate roots of the refusal to face the meaning of human finitude are found in the pride and rebellion of man. Some have made a declaration of independence from God. They believe they are self-sufficient in knowledge. Through the unaided human mind they can answer all questions that can be answered, and solve all problems that can be solved. There is no need for the divine revelation. It would be a blow to the pride of man which says that unaided human reason is sufficient....

For example, in our day Thomas J.J. Altizer has declared that God is dead. This was decreed by the pride of man. In his pride, Altizer maintained that man must be autonomous. He must be free to create his own nature and to formulate his own moral laws. If God is, and if God created man, man is not autonomous. He is not free to create his own nature, nor can he be left to his own will and whims as to what is right or wrong. He is not free to live his own life without being accountable to God. In his pride, Altizer wanted none of these things, so he decreed that God is dead in order that he might be free to live as it pleases him without being accountable to God. The arrogant heart cannot furnish fertile soil for seeds of truth... (1976, p. 73).

Bales' last statement—that "the arrogant heart cannot furnish fertile soil for seeds of truth"—is thoroughly biblical. Christ Himself warned: "For from within, out of the heart of men, evil thoughts proceed, fornications, thefts, murders, adulteries, covetings, wickednesses, deceit, lasciviousness, an evil eye, railing, **pride**, foolishness" (Mark 7:21-22, emp. added). The apostle John wrote: "For all that is in the world—the lust of the flesh, the lust of the eyes, and the **pride of life**—is not of the Father but is of the world" (1 John 2:16, NKJV, emp. added).

Somewhere in time, Altizer lost his way. In his pride, **finite** man sought to rid himself of the **infinite** God. He also forgot (if, indeed, he ever knew) that "Pride goeth before destruction, and a haughty spirit before a fall. Better it is to be of a lowly spirit with the poor, than to divide the spoil with the proud" (Proverbs 16: 18-19). Henry Morris has observed:

> The root of all sin...is the twin sin of unbelief and pride—the refusal to submit to God's will as revealed by His own Word and the accompanying assertion of self-sufficiency which enthrones the creature and his own will in the place of God (1971, pp. 214-215).

Imagine the position in which the devout unbeliever finds himself. He may be thinking: "I've been an unbeliever for a long time. If I alter my views now, I will lose face. My reputation is linked to my views. So is my conduct. Were I to change my mind, I would be condemning my whole past existence and altering my entire future life—in both word and deed."

Difficult scenario, to be sure. Not only is pride heavily involved, but personal integrity as well. Perhaps this is the very thing that Jesus had in mind when He said: "Anyone who **resolves** to do the will of God will know whether the teaching is from God" (John 7:17, NRSV, emp. added). If a person so desires, he or she **can** replace unbelief with belief. As the apostle John brought the book of Revelation to a close, he wrote: "He that will, let him take the water of life freely" (Revelation 22:17). The operative phrase here, of course, is "he that will." It is one thing to let pride **get** in the way; it is entirely another to let it **remain** there.

Immorality

In his book, *If There's a God, Why Are There Atheists?*, R.C. Sproul titled one of the chapter subheadings "The Threat of Moral Excellence." In that section, he noted:

> It is a common occurrence among social human beings that a person who manifests a superior excellence is resented by his contemporaries. The student who consistently breaks the curve of the academic grading system is frequently treated with quiet hostility by his classmates.... The unusually competent person represents a threat not only to his peers but to his superiors as well, and is frequently treated as persona non grata.... **Competency at a moral level is perhaps the most unwelcome kind of competency** (1978, pp. 94,95, emp. added).

Who among us has not endured taunts from associates because we steadfastly refused to participate in something immoral? Think about the teenager who rebuffs his friends' invitation to "do drugs," the employee who chooses not to "fudge" his time sheet, or the college student who elects not to cheat on the exam. Those who **are willing** to participate in immoral acts often react in hostile fashion to those who **are not**.

Consider the case of Jesus Christ. When He calmed the storm-tossed seas in Matthew 8, those around Him asked, "What manner of man is this?" (vs. 27). When those sent to spy on Him reported to the chief priests and Pharisees who had commissioned them, they admitted: "Never man so spake" (John 7:47). Christ was **morally** unique. He was the One Who taught:

> Ye have heard that it was said, "An eye for an eye, and a tooth for a tooth": but I say unto you, resist not him that is evil: but whosoever smiteth thee on thy right cheek, turn to him the other also. And if any man would go to law with thee, and take away thy coat, let him have thy cloak also. And whosoever shall compel thee to go one mile, go with him two.... I say unto you, love your enemies, and pray for them that persecute you (Matthew 5:38-41,44)

Practically everything Christ taught, and did, was in contradistinction to the common practices of His day—and of ours. As Sproul has suggested:

> The unique moral excellence of Jesus was a massive threat to His contemporaries, particularly to those who were considered to be the moral elite of His day. It was the Pharisees (those "set apart" to righteousness) who were most hostile to Jesus. Though the popular masses hailed the Pharisees for their moral excellence, Jesus exposed them as hypocrites. He "broke their curve," providing a new standard under which the old standard of morality dissolved. Jesus disintegrated the firm security of His contemporaries. **When the Holy appeared, the pseudo-holy were exposed** (1978, pp. 95-96, emp. added, parenthetical comment in orig.).

Little wonder, then, that "the chief priests and the scribes sought how they might put him to death" (Luke 22:2).

Now, multiply this angry attitude throughout a human race, the majority of which has become so vile that "it is written, 'There is none righteous, no, not one; there is none that understandeth, there is none that seeketh after God'" (Romans 3:10-11). If people reacted with downright disgust to the moral perfection of God's personal representative here on Earth, with what kind of dastardly disdain might they be expected to react to the moral perfection of the God Who inhabits eternity?

In his 1910 book, *Man's Need of God*, historian David Smith lamented not only the sorry state in which mankind found itself, but the fact that "[i]t is not intellectual aberration but moral depravity—the blight of uncleanness, the canker of corruption" that has brought humans to the precipice of moral bankruptcy (p. 98). One need not look long or hard to find corroborating evidence for such an assessment. For example, Aldous Huxley admitted:

> **I had motives for not wanting the world to have meaning**; consequently, assumed it had none, and was able without any difficulty to find satisfying reasons for this assumption.... The philosopher who finds no meaning in

the world is not concerned exclusively with a problem in pure metaphysics; he is also concerned to prove there is no valid reason why he personally should not do as he wants to do.... For myself, as no doubt for most of my contemporaries, **the philosophy of meaninglessness was essentially an instrument of liberation**. The liberation we desired was simultaneously liberation from a certain political and economic system and **liberation from a certain system of morality. We objected to the morality because it interfered with our sexual freedom** (1966, 3:19, emp. added).

Huxley's admission leaves little to the imagination. Why did he, and so many of his contemporaries, abandon belief in God? It was to: (a) avoid the objective moral standards laid down by Heaven; and (b) provide legitimacy for indiscriminate sexual behavior of a wanton nature. In fact, this is one of the primary planks in the platform of modern-day humanism.

In the area of sexuality, we believe that intolerant attitudes, often cultivated by orthodox religions and puritanical cultures, unduly repress sexual conduct. The right to birth control, abortion, and divorce should be recognized. While we do not approve of exploitive, denigrating forms of sexual expression, neither do we wish to prohibit, by law or social sanction, sexual behavior between consenting adults. The many varieties of sexual exploration should not in themselves be considered "evil." Without countenancing mindless permissiveness or unbridled promiscuity, a civilized society should be a **tolerant** one. Short of harming others or compelling them to do likewise, individuals should be permitted to express their sexual proclivities and pursue their life-styles as they desire (*Humanist Manifestos I & II*, 1973, pp. 18-19, emp. in orig.)

It should come as no surprise, then, that "as man finds himself self-sufficient he will discard his religious convictions, or having none, he will fight those of others" (Smith, 1974, pp. 152-153). The psalmist addressed this very point when he wrote: "The fool hath said in his heart, 'There is no God.' **They are corrupt, they have done abominable works**; There is none that doeth good" (14:1, emp. added).

Some might object on the grounds that not **all** unbelievers lapse into moral decay. Bales addressed this objection in his book, *How Can Ye Believe?*

> First, men are sometimes glad to get away from the moral authority of the Christian faith not because they want to do some things that it forbids, but **because some of the things which it sanctions and commands they do not want to do**. Second, the sinful attitude of heart may not be of the type that we generally associate with immorality, but such as the pride of individuals who do not want to admit that they are a long way from what they ought to be. Such an individual may welcome unbelief because it removes from his sight the accusing high standard of the faith which passes judgment on his life.... Third, the collapse in moral conduct may not come immediately because...the habits of the individual and his attitudes have been constructed by Christian morality and he finds it difficult to break away from them and to get over the idea of the shamefulness of certain types of conduct.... Fourth, it has not been suggested that this is the **only** cause of unbelief (1976, pp. 99,100, emp. added).

As this section on immorality as a cause of unbelief draws to a close, I believe it is appropriate to conclude with the following quotation from Wilbur M. Smith:

> The point I am making is this: one of the reasons why men refuse to accept the Christian Faith is because the very principles of their lives are in every way contradictory to the ethical principles of the Bible, and, **determined to remain in the lawlessness of their own sensuality**, they could not possibly embrace a holy religion nor walk with a holy God, nor look for salvation to His holy Son, nor have any love for His holy Word. ...**one of the deepest, profoundest, most powerful causes for unbelief**, holding men back from Christ **is a life of sin** (1974, p. 170, emp. added).

Scientific Materialism

Let's face it. We are living in an era where science reigns supreme and where we view daily its astonishing accomplishments.

Today, citizens of most civilized countries are better fed, better clothed, and healthier than they ever have been. Science has increased life spans, improved planetary transportation, and altered forever methods of global communication. It has eradicated smallpox and is on the verge of eliminating polio. Scientific research has improved radically such things as educational, medical, and recreational facilities, especially when compared to those of previous generations. It even stands at the brink of decoding the entire human genome.

Pretty impressive stuff, to say the least. And therein lies the problem. Because of the tremendous strides that have been, and are being, made, science has become somewhat of a sacred cow and the laboratory a sort of "holy of holies." As Smith put it:

> The very word "laboratory" has in it the connotation of certainty, of wonder, of the discovery of secrets. Millions of people are living today because of the development of medicine, and thank God for that! Many are able to walk the streets today because of insulin, who, otherwise, would long ago have been in their graves. One discovery drives men on to another. The eliciting of one secret is only the opening of the door into another realm of mystery and delight. There is a positiveness, definiteness, and promise about mathematical equations, physical laws, and chemical formulae, which make men feel that here their feet are on solid rock, that their minds are grappling with realities (1974, pp. 162-163).

While we should be grateful for the strides that science has made, we also should acknowledge all that science owes to God. During a seminar on origins at Murray, Kentucky on November 29, 1980, Russell C. Artist, former chairman of the biology department and professor emeritus at David Lipscomb University, commented: "The statement, 'In the beginning God created the heavens and the earth,' is the cornerstone of all scientific thinking." Dr. Artist was doing what far too many scientists are unwilling to do —"give credit where credit is due." If Genesis 1:1 is the **cornerstone** of science, then surely Genesis 1:28—wherein man is commanded to "subdue and have dominion over" the Earth—is the **charter** of science.

Yet undoubtedly one of the greatest obstacles to belief in God is the attitude that science somehow has made belief in God obsolete. Philosopher A.J. Ayer put it this way: "I believe in science. That is, I believe that a theory about the way the world works is not acceptable unless it is confirmed by the facts, and I believe that **the only way to discover what the facts are is by empirical observation"** (1966, p. 13, emp. added). Or, as humanistic philosopher Paul Kurtz suggested: "To adopt such a scientific approach unreservedly is to accept as ultimate in all matters of fact and real existence the appeal to the evidence of **experience alone; a court subordinate to no higher authority**, to be overridden by no prejudice however comfortable" (1973, p. 109, emp. added).

At the conclusion of the third annual Conference on Science and Philosophy and Religion in Their Relation to the Democratic Way of Life, a formal statement was framed to summarize the participants' conclusions. In that statement was this declaration:

> A world which has gained a unique sense of power through its inventive ability and its scientific knowledge, which has been trained to think in concrete terms and their immediate ends, and which enjoys the thrill of a continually changing panorama of obtainable knowledge is peculiarly resistant to the teachings of religion with its emphasis on ultimate objectives, and absolute truths (as quoted in Smith, 1974, p. 152).

In commenting on this assessment, Wilbur M. Smith wrote: "The result of such preoccupations is the snuffing out, as it were, of spiritual thoughts, or, a turning away from spiritual values. **Material contentment often makes for spiritual indifference**" (1974, p. 160, emp. added). Edward Watkin, in his book, *Theism, Agnosticism and Atheism*, opined:

> Man today is fixing his attention wholly upon a horizontal plane to the exclusion of the vertical. As this movement of exclusive outlook, this naturalism and religious humanism, has grown in power and self-confidence, it has produced

an increasing blindness to religious truth. Those whose minds it has formed, and they are the majority of civilized mankind today, have their attention fixed so exclusively upon the phenomena visible along the **horizontal** line of vision that they can no longer see the spiritual realities visible only in the depths by a **vertical** direction... (1936, pp. 23-24, emp. added).

Approximately two decades after Dr. Watkin made that statement, its truthfulness was borne out by a prominent member of the scientific community. While attending the Darwinian Centennial Convocation at the University of Chicago in 1958, Sir Julian Huxley stated that, so far as he was concerned, Darwinian science had "removed the whole idea of God as the creator of organisms from the sphere of rational discussion" (1960, p. 45). After almost another four decades had passed, evolutionist Richard Lewontin expressed even more forcefully the unbeliever's attitude toward both science and God.

Our willingness to accept scientific claims against common sense is the key to an understanding of the real struggle between science and the supernatural. We take the side of science **in spite** of the patent absurdity of some of its constructs, **in spite** of it failure to fulfill many of its extravagant promises of health and life, **in spite** of the tolerance of the scientific community for unsubstantiated just-so stories, because we have a prior commitment, a commitment to naturalism. It is not that the methods and institutions of science somehow compel us to accept a material explanation of the phenomenal world, but, on the contrary, that **we are forced by our *a priori* adherence to material causes** to create an apparatus of investigation and a set of concepts that produce material explanations, no matter how counter-intuitive, no matter how mystifying to the uninitiated. Moreover, **that materialism is absolute, for we cannot allow a Divine Foot in the door** (1997, p. 31, emp. in orig. except for last two sentences).

Notice what Lewontin has admitted. Neither he, nor his scientific cohorts, bases unbelief on "the methods and institutions" of science. Rather they are "forced" by their "*a priori* adherence to material causes" to accept an absolute materialism. Why? Because they resolutely refuse to "allow a Divine Foot in the door." Thus, scientific materialism has fostered unbelief.

In his book, *Intellectuals Don't Need God and Other Modern Myths*, Alister E. McGrath asked: "But what of the idea that science has rendered God unnecessary? As scientific understanding advances, will not God be squeezed out from the gaps in which Christian apologists have tried to lodge him?" (1993, p. 166). While Dr. McGrath expressed hope that this will not happen, he likewise acknowledged that, in fact, all too often it has. Smith wrote:

> But **science is no synonym for spirituality**, and the life of men is made up of more things than can be measured with test tubes and balances. Yet, man is so absorbed in the pursuit of nature's secrets that he is increasingly ignorant of his inner spiritual life, and this is one of the tragedies of our day. Men engaged in science are themselves partly to blame for this. They devote days and nights, months, and sometimes years, to the discovery of some scientific fact, but they will not give twenty minutes a day to pondering the Word of God, nor five minutes a day to the exercise of their soul in prayer to God.... Of course if men are going to lift such a miserable thing as humanity to a pedestal, then a holy and invisible God must be not only ignored, but despisingly rejected and hated, which is why many of our intellectual leaders today who look upon **humanity** as divine, must irritatingly and scornfully declare their conviction that a transcendent, omnipotent, sovereign and eternal Being can, for them, have no meaning (1974, pp. 163,164, emp. added).

Intellectual Intimidation

Some time ago, I received a heart-rending letter from a young Christian who was a graduate student in the applied sciences at a state university. His major professor was a man he termed "a giant in his field...rocket-scientist intelligent...and a devout evolutionist." In his letter, the student went on to say:

Working this closely with one who thinks as he does is beginning to cause not a small amount of cognitive dissonance in my own mind. Hundreds of thousands of scientists
can't be wrong, can they? Consensual validation cannot be
pushed aside in science. How can that many people be following a flag with no carrier, and someone not find out? **I
do not want to be a fool!**

This young writer expressed what many people experience,
yet are unable to enunciate so eloquently. It is not an enjoyable experience to be exposed to the slings and barbs of infidelity. Nor is
it pleasant to be labeled as dumb, stupid, or ignorant because you
hold to a belief different than your opponent's. Yet it is those
very labels that have been applied to those of us who are willing
to defend the existence of God or the concept of creation. Several
years ago, the famous atheist/evolutionist of Oxford University,
Richard Dawkins wrote: "It is absolutely safe to say that if you meet
somebody who claims not to believe in evolution, that person is
ignorant, stupid, or **insane** (or **wicked,** but I'd rather not consider that)" (1989a, p. 34, emp. added). The old adage, "Sticks
and stones may break my bones, but words can never hurt me,"
may be easy to parrot in such instances, but it is difficult to believe and does not offer much comfort. Truth be told, words **do**
hurt. No one enjoys being thought of (or actually called) ignorant,
stupid, insane, or wicked.

In this day and age, it is increasingly common to encounter
those who once knew what they believed and why they believed
it, yet who end up dazed, confused, and faithless because they have
been intimidated intellectually. The "cognitive dissonance" men-
tioned by the young man is the label for the internal struggle one
experiences when presented with new information that contra-
dicts what he believes to be true. As the student struggled for
consistency, he realized that he had only two choices. He either
had to: (1) alter what he previously believed; or (2) disregard the
new information being presented to him by "a rocket-scientist intelligent" professor whom he respected. This young Christian—

like so many before and after him—once knew what he believed, and why. But by the time his letter arrived in my office, he no longer knew either. He pleaded: "I am a confused young man with some serious questions about my mind, my faith, and my God. Please help me."

That agonizing plea—"please help me"—has been echoed countless times through the centuries by those who languish in the "cognitive dissonance" that results from replacing the wisdom of God with the wisdom of man. The young graduate student asked: "Hundreds of thousands of scientists can't be wrong, can they?" This question may be addressed as follows. First, any argument based on "counting heads" is fallacious. Philosophy professors instruct their students on the various fallacies of human thought, one of which is the "fallacy of consensus." In his book, *Fundamentals of Critical Thinking*, atheistic philosopher Paul Ricci discussed the "argument from consensus," and explained in detail its errors (1986, p. 175). Interestingly, however, in the pages immediately prior to his discussion, Ricci had offered the following as a "proof" of evolution: "The reliability of evolution not only as a theory but as a principle of understanding is not contested by **the vast majority** of biologists, geologists, astronomers, and other scientists" (1986, p. 172, emp. added).

Mr. Ricci thus fell victim to the very fallacy about which he tried to warn his readers—i.e., **truth is not determined by popular opinion or majority vote**. A thing may be, and often is, true even when accepted only by a small minority. The history of science is replete with such examples. British medical doctor, Edward Jenner (1749-1823), was scorned when he suggested smallpox could be prevented by infecting people with a less-virulent strain of the disease-causing organism. Yet his vaccine has helped eradicate smallpox. Dr. Ignaz Semmelweis (1818-1865) of Austria is another interesting case study. He noticed the high mortality rate among surgical patients and suggested that the deaths resulted from surgeons washing neither their hands nor their instruments between patients. Dr. Semmelweis asked them to do both, but they ridiculed him and refused to comply (thereby endangering the lives of thousands of patients). Today, the solutions posed by this gentle doctor are the basis of antiseptic techniques in surgery.

Scientific successes often have occurred **because** researchers rebelled against the status quo. Sometimes "consensual validation" must be set aside—**for the sake of truth**. The cases of Jenner and Semmelweis document all too well the fact that "the intellectuals," although in the majority, may be wrong. Just because "hundreds of thousands of scientists" believe something does not make it right. As Darrell Huff observed: "People can be wrong in the mass, just as they can individually" (1959, p. 122). If something is true, stating it a million times does not make it any truer. Similarly, if something is false, stating it a million times does not make it true.

Second, the prestige of a position's advocates has nothing to do with whether that position is true or false. Newspaper magnate William Randolph Hurst, Jr. once wrote about pressures from "fashionable ideas...which are advanced with such force that common sense itself becomes the victim." He observed that a person under such pressure then may act "with an irrationality which is almost beyond belief" (1971, p. A-4).

As proof of his point, consider the suggestion some years ago by renowned scientist (and Nobel laureate) W.B. Shockley that highly intelligent women be artificially inseminated using spermatozoa from a select group of Nobel Prize winners in order to produce what he felt would be quite obviously super-intelligent offspring. There can be no doubt whatsoever that Dr. Shockley happened to be "a giant in his field" with "rocket scientist" intelligence. If the intellect or prestige of a person is enough to guarantee the validity of the positions he (or she) espouses, then perhaps the human race should have taken Dr. Shockley up on his suggestion.

But intellectual prowess or prestige does **not** confer veracity on a person's position(s). Shockley's idea, for example, was based on nothing more than the narcissism of an over-inflated ego. As Taylor has commented: "Status in the field of science is no guarantee of the truth" (1984, p. 226). The soundness or strength of a claim is not based on: (a) the number of people supporting the claim; or (b) the intellect or prestige of the one(s) making that claim.

Third, the idea of strict objectivity in intellectual circles is a myth. While most scholars like to think of themselves as broad-minded, unprejudiced paragons of virtue, the fact is that they, too, on occasion, suffer from bouts of bias, bigotry, and presuppositionalism. Nobel laureate James Watson remarked rather bluntly: "In contrast to the popular conception supported by newspapers and mothers of scientists, a goodly number of scientists are not only narrow-minded and dull, but also just stupid" (1968, p. 14). Phillip Abelson, one-time editor of *Science*, wrote: "One of the most astonishing characteristics of scientists is that some of them are plain, old-fashioned bigots. Their zeal has a fanatical, egocentric quality characterized by disdain and intolerance for anyone or any value not associated with a special area of intellectual activity" (1964, 144:373). No doubt the same could be said of intellectuals in other fields as well (e.g., philosophy, business, the arts, etc.).

Fourth, on occasion it has been the "intellectuals" who have championed what can only be called "crazy" concepts. Bales addressed this fact when he wrote:

> There is no unreasonable position, there is no weird idea, which has not been propagated by some brilliant man who has a number of degrees after his name. Some have argued that everything is an illusion, others have maintained that they are nothing but a mess of matter or just a living mass of meat, others maintain that there is no realm of the rational and thus the very concept of an intellectual is an illusion...
> (1976, p. 91).

Space would fail me were I to try to provide a comprehensive listing of the "weird" ideas proposed by those esteemed as "intellectuals." For example, the eminent astrophysicist of Great Britain, Sir Fred Hoyle, proposed in his book, *Evolution from Space,* that life was planted here by creatures from outer space, and that insects are their representatives here on Earth (1981, p. 127). The celebrated philosopher René Descartes, in his *Meditations on First Philosophy* (1641), propounded the view that it is impossible to **know** anything (which makes one want to ask, "How does he **know** that it is impossible to **know**?"). And so on.

The majority ultimately will abandon God's wisdom in favor of their own. But the wisdom with which we **are** impressed is not always the wisdom with which we **should be** impressed. Christ, in His Sermon on the Mount, warned that "narrow is the gate and difficult is the way which leads to life, and there are few who find it" (Matthew 7:14). Guy N. Woods observed that this injunction

> ...was designed to guard the Lord's people from the corrupting influences of an evil environment, as well as from the powerful appeals of mob psychology to which so many in every generation succumb.... Man, by nature, is a social and gregarious being, tending to flock or gather together with others of his kind.... Man may, and often does, imbibe the evil characteristics of those about him as readily, and often more so, than the good ones (1982, 124[1]:2).

When the apostle Paul penned his first epistle to the Christians in Corinth, he warned:

> For it is written, I will destroy the wisdom of the wise, and the discernment of the discerning will I bring to naught. Where is the wise? Where is the scribe? Where is the disputer of this world? Hath not God made foolish the wisdom of the world? For seeing that in the wisdom of God the world through its wisdom knew not God, it was God's good pleasure through the foolishness of preaching to save them that believe (1 Corinthians 1:19-21).

It should not surprise us that many "intelligent" people view belief in God as the fool's way out. Paul also commented that

> not many wise after the flesh, not many mighty, not many
> noble, are called: but God chose the foolish things of the
> world, that he might put to shame them that are wise; and
> God chose the weak things of the world, that he might put
> to shame the things that are strong (1 Corinthians 1:26-27).

The most intelligent often are the least spiritual because "the god
of this world" (2 Corinthians 4:3-4) has blinded their minds.

We must not fall prey to mob psychology which suggests because "everyone is doing it" that somehow makes it right. The graduate student said, "I do not want to be a fool." It was a joy to tell
him that he does not have to bear that stigma because "The fool
hath said in his heart, there is no God" (Psalm 14:1). We need not
be intimidated by the pseudo-intellectualism of those who esteem themselves with higher regard than they do their Creator.
Lucy, the character in the *Peanuts* cartoon, was correct when
she told Charlie Brown, "You're not right; you just **sound** right!"

Evil, Pain, and Suffering

Surely it can be said without fear of contradiction that one of
the most frequent, and thus one of the most important, causes of
unbelief is the existence of evil, pain, and suffering in the world.
But before we explore this concept, let us take a momentary di-
version to separate the **genuine** problem from the **counterfeit**.
When an individual claims not to believe in God because of the
problem of evil, pain, and suffering, the person **making** such a
claim may mean something entirely different than what the person **hearing** the claim thinks he means. Allow me to explain.

Admittedly, some people have difficulty believing in God because of what they consider to be **real intellectual obstacles**
to such a belief. *Ex nihilo* creation, a virgin birth, or the bodily
resurrection of Christ from the dead cause some to consider belief in God on par with belief in the Tooth Fairy or Santa Claus.
Such concepts represent insurmountable barriers to the ultimate
acceptance of God's existence.

Other people, however, face no such intellectual obstacles. Instead, they simply do not want to have to deal with the issue of the ultimate existence of a transcendent God. Their refusal to believe is not based necessarily on "this" barrier or "that" barrier. Rather, belief in God simply is inconvenient at best, or bothersome at worst. In a chapter titled "What Keeps People from Becoming Christians?" in his timely book, *Intellectuals Don't Need God*, Alister McGrath exerted considerable effort in an attempt to separate the claims of these two types of individuals when he wrote:

> "I could never be a Christian because of the problem of suffering" can mean two quite different things: (a) Having thought the matter through carefully, it seems to me that there is a real problem posed to the intellectual coherence of the Christian faith because of the existence of human suffering; (b) I don't want to get involved in a discussion about Christianity, which could get very personal and threatening. But I don't want to admit this, as it might seem to imply that I lack intellectual courage, stamina, or honesty. I can save face by letting it be understood that there are good grounds for my rejection of Christianity. So let me select a problem...suffering will do very nicely. Anyway, it will stall the efforts of this guy who's trying to convert me.

> For some, then, throwing intellectual problems at the Christian evangelist is like a warplane ejecting flares to divert heat-seeking missiles. It is a decoy meant to divert a deadly attack. But intellectual difficulties nevertheless constitute a real problem for some people, and answers must be given to their difficulties (1993, pp. 64-65, ellipsis in orig.).

It is not my intention in this section to deal with those in the second category who use the problem of evil, pain, and suffering merely as a ruse to hide their own cowardice in the face of overwhelming evidence regarding the existence of God. Likely, no evidence ever could convince them. They fall into the same category as Goethe, who said: "A voice from heaven would not convince me...that a woman gives birth without knowing man, and that a dead man rises from the grave" (as quoted in Smith, 1974, p. 175). Rather, I would like to discuss the unbelief of those who fall into the first category—i.e., people who view the co-existence of God and moral evil as an intellectual inconsistency that is incapable of being solved. Their number is legion, and their tribe is increasing.

. For example, consider the following assessments offered by a variety of writers that runs the gamut from a Nobel laureate to a former well-known televangelist. The Nobel laureate is Steven Weinberg, author of *Dreams of a Final Theory*, which includes a chapter titled "What About God?" Within that chapter these comments can be found.

> I have to admit that sometimes nature seems more beautiful than strictly necessary. Outside the window of my home office there is a hackberry tree, visited frequently by a convocation of politic birds: blue jays, yellow-throated vireos, and, loveliest of all, an occasional red cardinal. Although I understand pretty well how brightly colored feathers evolved out of a competition for mates, it is almost irresistible to imagine that all this beauty was somehow laid on for our benefit. **But the God of birds and trees would have to be also the God of birth defects and cancer....**
>
> Remembrance of the Holocaust leaves me unsympathetic to attempts to justify the ways of God to man. **If there is a God that has special plans for humans, then He has taken very great pains to hide His concern for us** (1993, pp. 250-251, emp. added).

The former well-known televangelist is Charles B. Templeton, a high school dropout who, according to one writer, has "the natural flare and fluidity of a salesman" (Lockerbie, 1998, p. 228). He served for many years as the pulpit minister for the Avenue Road Church (Toronto, Ontario, Canada) where his ubiquitous "Youth for Christ" rallies in the late 1940s were extremely popular. Eventually he became a world-renowned evangelist with the Billy Graham Crusade. Then, one day, he quit. He abandoned it all—not just the Billy Graham Crusade, but belief in God, belief in Christ, belief in the Bible, belief in heaven—everything! He explained why in his book, *Farewell to God*.

I was ridding myself of archaic, outdated notions. I was dealing with life as it is. There would be an end to asking the deity for his special interventions on my behalf because I was one of the family.... If there is a loving God, why does he permit—much less create—earthquakes, droughts, floods, tornadoes, and other natural disasters which kill thousands of innocent men, women, and children every year? How can a loving, omnipotent God permit—much less create—encephalitis, cerebral palsy, brain cancer, leprosy, Alzheimer's and other incurable illnesses to afflict millions of men, women, and children, most of whom are decent people? (1996, pp. 221,230).

Almost a decade-and-a-half earlier, B.C. Johnson had given expression to the same kinds of concerns in *The Atheist Debater's Handbook*.

A house catches on fire and six-month-old baby is painfully burned to death. Could we possibly describe as 'good' any person who had the power to save this child and yet refused to do so? God undoubtedly has the power and yet... he has refused to help. Can we call God "good"? (1983, p 99).

It is not my intention here to provide an in-depth response to these (or similar) accusations. These matters have been dealt with elsewhere in detail (see: Jackson, 1988; Major, 1998; Thompson, 1990, 1993; Thompson and Jackson, 1992). Instead, I merely would like to document the role that evil, pain, and suffering have played, and still continue to play, as an important cause of man's unbelief.

Many have been those who, through the ages, have abandoned their belief in God because of the presence of evil, pain, and suffering in their lives or in the lives of those close to them. Earlier, I documented how, in 1851, Charles Darwin abandoned once and for all any vestige of belief in God after the death of his oldest daughter, Annie (see Desmond and Moore, 1991, pp. 384, 386-387). But Darwin was not the only one so affected. Nine years later, on September 15, 1860, Thomas Huxley was to watch his oldest son, four-year-old Noel, die in his arms from scarlet fever. In their massive, scholarly biography, *Darwin*, Desmond and Moore wrote that Noel's death brought Huxley "...to the edge of a breakdown. Huxley tried to rationalize the 'holy leave-taking' as he stood over the body, with its staring blue eyes and tangled golden hair, **but the tragedy left a deep scar**" (1991, p. 503, emp. added).

At Noel's funeral, the minister briefly referred to 1 Corinthians 15:14-19 in his eulogy. When he quoted the passage from that section of Scripture which mentions, "if the dead be not raised," Huxley was outraged. Eight days after Noel's death, on September 23, he wrote to his close friend, Charles Kingsley, about the minister's words: "I cannot tell you how inexpressibly they shocked me. [The preacher—BT] had neither wife nor child, or he must have known that his alternative involved a blasphemy against all that was best and noblest in human nature. I could have laughed with scorn" (see Leonard Huxley, 1900, 1:151-152). In the equally scholarly (and equally massive) companion biography that he authored, *Huxley*, Adrian Desmond wrote of the man known as "Darwin's Bulldog" on the day of his son's death:

> He sat in the study facing the tiny body. His emotions were unleashed as he looked back to that New Year's Eve 1856, when he had sat at the same desk and pledged on his son's birth to give "a new and healthier direction to all Biological Science." He had found redemption on his son's death. There was no blame, **only submission to Nature**, and that brought its own catharsis (1997, p. 287, emp. added).

"Submission to Nature" became Huxley's watchword. Belief in God—however feeble it may have been prior to Noel's death—now had evaporated completely. All that remained was to give "a new and healthier direction to all Biological Science." And so it was to "Nature" that Huxley devoted the remainder of his life.

But not all such events have occurred in centuries long since gone. Modern-day parallels abound. Samuel Langhorne Clemens (a.k.a. Mark Twain) became implacably embittered against God after the death, in 1896, of his favorite daughter, Suzy. Famed English novelist, W. Somerset Maugham, recounted in his autobiography, *The Summing Up*, how that as a youngster he had prayed to God one night that he might be delivered from the terrible speech impediment that afflicted him. The next day he arose, only to find that the impediment still was present. So profound was his grief and disappointment at the failure of God to cure him overnight that from that point forward he pledged never to believe in God again.

In the mid-1960s, a devoutly religious young man from Chattanooga, Tennessee was a role model for all of his classmates. He led a prayer group, and planned to become a foreign missionary —until his sister died of leukemia and his father committed suicide. The boy's belief in God collapsed, and he subsequently became one of America's most outspoken unbelievers, humanists, and pro-abortion advocates. That boy's name?—Ted Turner, founder of world-famous CNN, the Turner Broadcasting System, and other well-known media enterprises.

But, of course, it is not just the famous who abandon their belief in God because of evil, pain, and suffering in their lives. The "man (or woman, as the case may be) on the street" is no less affected. A case in point is that of Judith Hayes, a senior writer for *The American Rationalist*. In 1996, Mrs. Hayes authored an acrimonious tirade titled, *In God We Trust: But Which One?*, in which she explained why she left the Lutheran Church (Missouri Synod) and became an atheist. First, as a youngster she had a good friend named Susan who was a devout Buddhist. Judith, however, simply could not accept the teachings of Scripture that Susan would be lost if she did not obey the biblical scheme of redemption set forth so plainly in God's Word. Thus she made, not a rational decision based upon the evidence, but an emotional decision based on her own "inner desires." Neither Christianity, she said, nor its God, could be accepted as true.

Second, Judith eventually married. But the relationship soured and disintegrated due to the fact, Mrs. Hayes reported, that her husband became verbally abusive. Instead of considering the possibility that **she** had made a poor choice of mates, or that **her husband** had misused his own personal freedom of choice, Judith blamed God. "[H]ow could I possibly have wound up married to a tyrant?," she wrote. "Why had God forsaken me?" (1996, p. 15).

Again, time and space would fail me were I to attempt merely to enumerate, much less discuss, all those who have abandoned belief in God because of evil, pain, and suffering in their lives or in the lives of those close to them. But what shall we say in regard to their accusations against their Creator? How shall we respond to their recalcitrant charge that—as a result of such epidemic, universal suffering—unbelief in God is both justifiable and justified?

Briefly, I would like to respond as follows. At the end of His six days of creation (Genesis 1:31), God surveyed all that He had made, and proclaimed it "very good" (Hebrew terminology representing that which was both complete and perfect). Pestilence, disease, and death among humans were unknown. Man existed in an idyllic paradise of happiness and beauty where he shared such an intimate and blissful covenant relationship with his Maker that God came to the garden "in the cool of the day" to commune with its human inhabitants (Genesis 3:8). Additionally, Genesis 3:22 records that man had continual access to the tree of life that stood in the garden, the fruit of which would allow him to live forever.

The peacefulness and tranquility of the first days of humanity were not to prevail, however. In Genesis 3—in fewer words than an average sportswriter would use to discuss a high school football game—Moses, through inspiration, discussed the breaking of the covenant relationship between man and God, the entrance of sin into the world, and the curse(s) that resulted therefrom. When our original parents revolted against their Creator, evil entered the world. Moses informs us that as a direct consequence of human sin, the Earth was "cursed" (Genesis 3:17). Paul, in Romans 8:19-20, declared that the entire creation was subjected to "vanity" and the "bondage of corruption" as a result of the sinful events that took place in Eden on that occasion. Things apparently deteriorated rapidly. Just three chapters later, Moses wrote:

> And Jehovah saw that the wickedness of man was great in the earth, and that every imagination of the thoughts of his heart was only evil continually. And it repented Jehovah that he had made man on the earth, and it grieved him at his heart. And Jehovah said, I will destroy man whom I have created from the face of the earth; both man and beast, and creeping things, and birds of the heavens... (Genesis 6:5-7).

From this assessment, one writer correctly concluded: "...the cause of all that is wrong with the earth is **not** godliness but rather **un**godliness" (Porter, 1974, p. 467, emp. in orig.). The matter of man's personal volition has much to do with this. The Scriptures speak to the fact that since God is love, and since love allows freedom of choice, God allows freedom of choice (cf. Joshua 24: 15; John 5:39-40). God did not create men and women as robots to serve Him slavishly without any kind of free moral agency on their part. Mankind now reaps the consequences of the misuse of freedom of choice (i.e., the sin) of previous generations. Surely one of the lessons taught here is that it does not pay to disobey the Creator. In his second epistle, Peter referred to "the world that then was," prior to its destruction by the Great Flood (3:6). That world no longer exists, however. Today we inhabit a once-perfect-but-now-flawed Earth. Man—not God—must bear the blame.

Furthermore, God created a world ruled by natural laws established at the Creation. If a man steps off the roof of a five-story building, gravity will pull him to the pavement beneath. If a boy steps in front of a moving freight train, since two objects cannot occupy the same space at the same time, the train will strike the child and likely kill him. The same laws that govern gravity, matter in motion, or similar phenomena also govern weather patterns, water movement, and other geological/meteorological conditions. **All** of nature is regulated by these laws—not just the parts that we find convenient. These natural laws are both inviolable and non-selective. **Everyone** (believer and unbeliever alike) must obey them or suffer the consequences. In Luke 13:2-5, Jesus told the story of eighteen men who perished when the tower of Siloam collapsed. Had these men perished because of their sin? No, they were no worse sinners than their peers. They died because a natural law was in force. Fortunately, natural laws work continually so that we can understand and benefit from them. We are not left to sort out some kind of haphazard system that works one day but not the next.

In the end, the most important question is not, "Why did 'this' or 'that' happen to me?," but instead, "How can I understand what has happened, and how am I going to react to it?" As McGrath put it:

> The sufferings of this earth are for real. They are painful. God is deeply pained by our suffering, just as we are shocked, grieved, and mystified by the suffering of our family and friends. But that is only half of the story. The other half must be told. It is natural that our attention should be fixed on what we experience and feel here and now. But faith demands that we raise our sights and look ahead to what lies ahead. We may suffer as we journey—but where are we going? What lies ahead? (1993, pp. 105-106).

As much as the unbeliever hates to admit it, there **are** times when suffering actually is **beneficial**. Think of the man whose chest begins to throb as he enters the throes of a heart attack. Think of the woman whose side begins to ache at the onset of acute appendicitis. Is it not true that pain often sends us to the doctor for prevention or cure? Is it not true also that at times suffering helps humankind develop the traits that people treasure the most? Bravery, heroism, altruistic love, self-sacrifice—all flourish in less-than-perfect environments, do they not? Yet people who exhibit such traits are cherished and honored as having gone "above and beyond the call of duty." Was this not the very point Christ was making when He said: "Greater love hath no man than this, that a man lay down his life for his friends" (John 15: 13)?

Instead of blaming God because evil, pain, and suffering exist, we should turn to Him for strength, and let tragedies, of whatever nature, remind us that this world never was intended to be a final home (Hebrews 11:13-16). Our time here is temporary (James 4:14), and with God's help, we are able to overcome whatever comes our way (Romans 8:35-39; Psalm 46:1-3). With Peter, the faithful believer can echo the sentiment that God, "who called you unto his eternal glory in Christ, after that ye have suffered a little while, shall himself perfect, establish, strengthen you" (1 Peter 5:10). As McGrath went on to say:

> Suffering and glorification are part of, but represent different stages in, the same process of growth in the Christian life. We are adopted into the family of God, we suffer, and we are glorified (Rom. 8:14-18). This is not an accidental relationship. They are all intimately connected within the overall pattern of Christian growth and progress toward the ultimate goal of the Christian life—being finally united with God and remaining with him forever.
>
> We are thus presented with a glorious vision of a new realm of existence. It is a realm in which suffering has been defeated. It is a realm pervaded by the refreshing presence of God, from which the presence and power of sin have finally be excluded. It lies ahead, and though we have yet to enter into it, we can catch a hint of its fragrance and hear its music in the distance. It is this hope that keeps us going in this life of sadness, which must end in death....
>
> It is here that the resurrection of Christ becomes of central importance. The Resurrection allows the suffering of Christ to be seen in the perspective of eternity. Suffering is not pointless but leads to glory. Those who share in the sufferings of Christ may, through the resurrection of Christ, know

what awaits them at the end of history. It is for this reason that Paul is able to declare with such confidence that "our present sufferings are not worth comparing with the glory of what will be revealed in us" (Rom. 8:18). This is no groundless hope, no arbitrary aspiration. It is a hard-headed realism, grounded in the reality of the suffering and resurrection of Christ and in the knowledge that faith binds believers to Christ and guarantees that we shall share in his heritage....

Just as suffering is real, so are the promises of God and the hope of eternal life. This is no spiritual anesthetic, designed merely to enable us to copy with life's sorrows while they last. The death and resurrection of Christ...are pledges, sureties, and guarantees that what has been promised will one day be brought to glorious realization. For the moment we struggle and suffer in sadness mingled with bewilderment. But one day all that will be changed for the people of God. "God himself will be with them; he will wipe away every tear from their eyes, and death shall be no more, neither shall there be mourning nor crying nor pain any more, for the former things have passed away" (Rev. 21:3-4).

In that hope, we go forward into life in faith. We may not know exactly where that faith will lead us. But we **do** know that, wherever we go, the God of all compassion goes ahead of us and journeys with us, consoling and reassuring us, until that day when we shall see him face to face, and know him just as he knows us (1993, pp. 106-107,105-106,108, emp. in orig.).

Finally, no one can suggest—justifiably—that suffering per se is contrary to the existence or goodness of God in light of the series of events that transpired at Calvary almost two thousand years ago. The fact that **even the Son of God**, was subjected to evil, pain, and suffering (Hebrews 5:8; 1 Peter 2:21ff.) shows conclusively that God loves and cares for His creation. He is not the unloving, angry, vengeful God depicted by atheism and infidelity. Rather, "while we were enemies, we were reconciled to God through the death of his Son, much more, being reconciled, shall we be saved by his life" (Romans 5:10). God could have abandoned us to our own sinful devices but instead, "God commendeth his own love toward us, in that, while we were yet sinners, Christ died for us" (Romans 5:8). The apostle John stated the matter beautifully when he wrote:

> Herein was the love of God manifested in us, that God hath sent his only begotten Son into the world that we might live through him. Herein is love, not that we loved God, but that he loved us, and sent his Son to be the propitiation for our sins (1 John 4:9-10).

The unbeliever, for reasons known only to himself, either is unable, or unwilling, to concede the love of God. That—not the current evil, pain, or suffering that he currently endures—is the greatest tragedy of his life.

Hypocrisy or Misconduct of Believers

As much as those of us who believe in God hate to admit it, the truth of the matter is that on occasion our own actions have the potential to drive others toward unbelief. Try as we might, we still make mistakes. And sometimes our errors are egregious. There always have been sad stories of graphic hypocrisy and sordid misconduct on the part of believers (witness the drama of Ananias and Sapphira in Acts 5). But those cases have not always been publicized in such a "global" fashion as they now are. Today, when Jimmy Swaggart is photographed in a midnight tryst with a prostitute, or when Jim Bakker is tried in a court of law and found guilty of fraud involving church funds, it is a dream come true for evening network television programs. And what self-respecting news anchor or late-night comedian can resist the temptation to point out that these indiscretions and crimes have been committed by "believers"? Juicy, salacious tidbits, these—made all the more prurient by the fact that they fly in the face of everything pure and holy that such people are supposed to emulate in their lives.

Such hypocrisy and misconduct are hard pills to swallow even for fellow believers. But put yourself in the place of the person who already is struggling with doubts not only about the **system** of belief, but about the **God behind the system**. From their vantage point, when the system "fails" (i.e., when its adherents are unable to conform to it successfully in their own lives), what, then, shall be said about the God behind the system? As Bales observed:

> The corruptions, or shortcomings, or the hypocrisy in the lives of some believers have been used to justify the rejection of Christianity. They are viewed as adequate samples of the faith, and since the samples are not good, the faith is viewed as bad (1976, p. 49).

The Proverbs writer emphasized: "Confidence in an unfaithful man in time of trouble is like a broken tooth, and a foot out of joint" (25:19).

The unfaithfulness, hypocrisy, or misconduct of a single believer can have severe repercussions not just for other believers, but for unbelievers as well. Such circumstances provide "grist for the mill" of those who continually are searching for what they consider to be legitimate reasons not to believe in God. Perhaps Paul had this in mind when he wrote his first epistle to the young evangelist Timothy, urging that his instructions be carried out so that there would be "no occasion to the adversary for reviling" (1 Timothy 5:14). When believers become hypocrites, it supplies ammunition for those who have set themselves against God. And oftentimes the seed of potential disbelief blossoms into the flower of full-fledged unbelief. History is filled with sad-but-true accounts of those who plunged headlong into the embracing arms of infidelity as the result of unpleasant experiences with believers. Two of the most prominent examples that come to mind are H.G. Wells (see Clark, 1945) and Thomas H. Huxley (see Clark, 1948).

While we readily acknowledge the devastating effect that can result from the hypocrisy and/or misconduct of believers, and while we make no attempt whatsoever to justify or excuse such conduct, at the same time we must recognize the fact that it is sheer folly to blame God for the blunders of humanity. Rejecting God because of hypocrisy in the lives of some of His followers can become a two-edged sword. It has been said that "hypocrisy is the tribute that vice pays to virtue." Put another way, it is contradictory for an unbeliever to attempt to justify his unbelief by pointing out hypocrisy in someone else. The very fact that the unbeliever is willing to label the believer a "hypocrite" proves that he is aware of the fact that the believer is not measuring up to the high standards of the system he professes to follow. By suggesting that a believer is a hypocrite, the unbeliever implies that there is a system of belief that, when properly adhered to, would legitimize the conduct of the believer. Bales put it this way:

> When an individual accuses another of being a hypocrite, he is appealing to a standard of integrity. He is saying that it is **wrong** to be a hypocrite.... Those who hold to a world view which justifies the acceptance of moral law can consistently oppose hypocrisy. Those whose world view rules out moral law cannot be consistent and accept a standard which says that hypocrisy is wrong (1976, p. 50, emp. added).

No one condemned hypocrisy more than the Son of God Himself when, in Matthew 23, He pronounced the well-known "seven woes" on the religious leaders of His day and condemned them for their own hypocrisy. Additionally, the point needs to be made that, on occasion, the label of "hypocrite" is misapplied.

> A person is not a hypocrite because he is weak, and fails at times in his struggle against evil. He is not a hypocrite because he never perfectly achieves the perfect standard of life. In fact, he would be a hypocrite if he claimed that he **had** arrived at perfection. One is not a hypocrite because he is inconsistent. One may not be aware of the contradiction in his life. He may not be conscious of a particular clash between his profession and his conduct. Because the tares and the wheat may look alike for awhile does not mean that the wheat is made up of tares.... **Because weeds spring up in a garden, does this mean they were planted by the gardener**? (Bales, 1976, p. 50, emp. added).

The psalmist wrote: "It is better to take refuge in Jehovah than to put confidence in man" (118:8). Oh, that the unbeliever could learn that lesson.

Unjust Acts Committed by
Believers in the Name of God

It has been said that perhaps the only thing that is consistent in this world is **in**consistency. Anyone who has tried to live according to a standard can attest to the fact that such a statement contains an element of truth. The refrain, "Ah, consistency, thou art a rare jewel," reverberates within the human soul on a daily basis. Likely, most people **want** to live a consistent (and, hopefully, a **consistently good**) life. But such a feat often falls under the category of "easier said than done." Especially is this true when the standard by which a person is attempting to live is itself a consistently high one.

Enter belief in God and His Word. Even when those of us who firmly believe in God, and who confidently accept the Bible as His inspired communication to mankind, strive diligently to conform our words and deeds to those set out in God's Word, we sometimes still fail. David, Israel's beloved king, was described as a man after God's "own heart" (1 Samuel 13:14), yet he committed adultery with Bathsheba and had her husband, Uriah, murdered (2 Samuel 11-12). Peter, one of the Lord's hand-chosen apostles, loved his Master dearly, yet denied Him publicly three times on the eve of His crucifixion (Matthew 26:34,69-75). Even the apostle Paul waged his own personal war against the frequent temptations to do evil rather than good. When he wrote to encourage the first-century Christians in Rome, he admitted:

> For the good which I would I do not: but the evil which I would not, that I practice. For I delight in the law of God after the inward man: but I see a different law in my members, warring against the law of my mind, and bringing me into captivity under the law of sin which is in my members (Romans 7:19,22-23).

Adding to the problem is the fact that we may be absolutely sincere in what we do or say, yet still be entirely wrong. For example, consider the case of Uzzah. God had instructed the Israelites in a most specific manner (Numbers 4:15,19-20) that they were not to touch the "holy things," among which was the Ark of the Covenant. In 2 Samuel, however, the story is told of the day that King David had the Ark loaded onto an oxcart in order to move it. During the trip, the text indicates that "the oxen stumbled." Uzzah reached to steady the Ark and the moment he touched it, God struck him dead (2 Samuel 6:6-8). There can be no doubt that Uzzah was sincere in his attempts to protect the Ark. But he was **sincerely wrong**. Note specifically the Bible's statement that "God smote him there **for his error**" (2 Samuel 6:7).

Unfortunately, throughout human history there have been those who have professed the high standard of Christianity, yet who have committed unjust acts in the name of God—acts that have been a blight to believers and a boon to unbelievers. For example, in the time period between A.D. 1095 and 1270, eight different crusades occurred, during which armies representing "Christendom" battled Muslims in and around Jerusalem to gain control of the "holy city" and force Mohammed's followers into submission to Christ.

In 1613, Galileo published his first musings about the possible truthfulness of the Copernican system of planetary movements (i.e., that the Earth moves around the Sun, not the reverse as the old, revered Ptolemaic system suggested). In 1616, a decree was issued by the Catholic Church that prevented Galileo from publishing any additional supportive evidence for his hypothesis. But in 1632, he published *Dialogue Concerning the Two Great World Systems—Ptolemaic and Copernican*. One year later, in 1633, he found himself in front of an Inquisition in Rome—which found him guilty of violating church doctrine (in spite of the fact that he had been right in his defense of Copernicus' views).

In modern times, we have witnessed things no less savory. In 1988, Salman Rushdie authored *The Satanic Verses*, a book that drew the ire of radical Iranian Muslim spiritual leader, Ayatollah Khomeini. On February 4, 1989 Khomeini issued a *fatwa* (religious decree) in the name of Allah (God), calling for the immediate assassination of Rushdie and offering a six-million-dollar reward to anyone carrying out the task successfully. Rushdie was forced to go into hiding in Britain, where he was given 'round-the-clock protection by Scotland Yard.

In Northern Ireland, Catholics and Protestants have battled each other for decades under the flags of their respective religions. Bullets rip through shopping centers and schoolyards. Snipers fire on passers-by. Innocent adults, teenagers, and children die by the hundreds—all in the name of God. In Yugoslavia, "Christian" Serbs depart on "search and destroy" missions in an effort to rout opposing Muslim forces. "Ethnic cleansing" is carried out— again, in God's name.

Or, to bring the matter closer to home, militants bomb abortion clinics, maiming and killing patients and staff alike. These same individuals declare "open season" on medical doctors who perform abortions, and these practitioners subsequently are shot dead as they stand at their kitchen window or get in their car to drive to work. All in the name of the God of heaven.

And the unbeliever's case is made for him as he witnesses what he views as unjust, heinous acts carried out by people who are supposed to live daily by the Golden Rule and by the Word of the God Who established that Rule. The reaction is as swift as it is adamant. How could a good God sanction such barbaric inhumanity? And why would anyone want to serve such a God? While the unbeliever continues to ponder such questions and witness such atrocities, the roots of his unbelief grow ever deeper.

How should the believer respond to these things? First, let us admit forthrightly that such things as the brutality of the Crusades, the murder of abortionists, or the ethnic cleansing of non-

Christians **are** unjust deeds that never should have occurred in the first place. The acts committed are abhorrent and the attitudes of those responsible are deplorable.

Neither God nor Christ ever has **forced** men to submit to the Divine Will. In fact, Christ specifically stated: "My kingdom is not of this world: **if** my kingdom were of this world, **then** would my servants fight" (John 18:36, emp. added). Nothing can justify the torture inflicted on so many Muslims during the Crusades in an attempt to "cram Christianity down their collective throats." And the very idea of eliminating through "ethnic cleansing" those who are considered by some to be "enemies" of God is as repugnant as it is contrary to God's nature. The same God Who said, "As ye would that men should do to you, do ye to them likewise" (Luke 6:31), also commanded:

> Love your enemies, do good to them that hate you, bless them that curse you, pray for them that despitefully use you To him that smiteth thee on the one cheek offer also the other; and from him that taketh away thy cloak withhold not thy coat also. Give to every one that asketh thee; and of him that taketh away thy goods ask them not again. And if ye love them that love you, what thank have ye? for even sinners love those that love them. And if ye do good to them that do good to you, what thank have ye? for even sinners do the same. And if ye lend to them of whom ye hope to receive, what thank have ye? Even sinners lend to sinners, to receive again as much. But love your enemies, and do them good, and lend, never despairing; and your reward shall be great, and ye shall be sons of the Most High: for he is kind toward the unthankful and evil (Luke 6:27-30,32-35).

Nor does God condone the lawlessness involved in such acts as bombing abortion clinics or killing doctors who perform abortions. The same God Who condemns the slaughter of unborn children via abortion (Proverbs 6:16-17) likewise condemns the illegal slaughter of those who wrongly murder such children (Matthew 10:19).

Second, it is unfair to blame God for unjust acts committed in His name by those who claim to believe in Him, yet who disobey His will. While a person may be sincere, he or she may be **sincerely wrong**. The fact that someone commits an act "in God's name" does not mean necessarily that the **act itself** is sanctioned by the One in Whose name it was committed. For example, when law-enforcement officers act "in the name of the law," but illegally and unjustly pistol-whip a suspect to obtain a coerced confession, or commit perjury under oath in order to "frame" a defendant, does the "law" bear the blame for their offenses? Certainly not! The law specifically **forbade** their actions. The fact that those actions were carried out "in the name of the law" does not reflect poorly on the law itself. An unjust act that stands in opposition to an objective moral standard does not impugn the standard. So should it be with God. Reprehensible acts carried out "in God's name" should not reflect upon the high moral standard of God Himself.

Third, in this context it is important to separate the **real** believer from the **counterfeit** believer. Just because someone **claims** to be a believer does not necessarily mean that he or she actually **is** a believer. But how is that distinction to be made? God warned:

> Beware of false prophets who come to you in sheep's clothing, but inwardly are ravening wolves. **By their fruits ye shall know them**. Do men gather grapes of thorns, or figs of thistles? Even so every good tree bringeth forth good fruit; but the corrupt tree bringeth forth evil fruit. A good tree cannot bring forth evil fruit, neither can a corrupt tree bring forth good fruit.... Therefore by their fruits ye shall know them (Matthew 7:15-20).

A counterfeit remains a counterfeit regardless of the fact that it **claims** (or even **appears**) to be genuine. Its genuineness is determined by whether or not it successfully matches the list of characteristics for that which actually **is** real—the "genuine article" as we so often call it. The same is true of those who believe in God. The genuineness of both their claim and their actions is determined by whether or not what they say and do matches the list of characteristics for **true believers**.

Consider two modern-day analogies. Everything done in the name of "science" is not scientific. When a scientist says that in his professional opinion a nuclear bomb should be dropped on a certain country, he is not speaking as a scientist. He may have degrees in science and may even wear a white laboratory coat while peering into a microscope. But the fact remains that there is nothing inherent in the scientific method that would allow someone to determine whether nuclear energy should be employed to destroy cancer cells or entire cities. This is a decision that science is not equipped to make because it falls far beyond the pale of the scientific method.

And, not everything done in the name of "morality" is moral. Surely, one of the saddest events in American history occurred between 1932 and 1972 when the U.S. Public Health Service sanctioned the "Tuskegee Experiments," in which 399 poor African American men from Macon County, Alabama—known to be infected with *Treponema pallidum* (the microorganism responsible for the dreaded venereal disease, syphilis)—were studied to determine the effects of this debilitating condition. The government doctors involved in the study never told the participants that they had syphilis. Nor did they obtain "informed consent" from the men for their experiments.

Even though the physicians knew that the disease was fatal if left untreated, and even though antibiotics were available that could have saved the lives of the test subjects, those subjects were denied access to such antibiotics. Instead, they were patronized, prodded, and poked in what can only be called one of the most shameful experiments ever perpetrated on Americans. What was the rationale offered in later years for the experiments, once the scheme finally was uncovered? Those responsible claimed that they wanted to provide knowledge of the disease in the hope that it might prevent the physical degradation and death so often associated with syphilis victims. And, of course, they wanted to secure information that could be used to slow, or halt, the "moral degradation" associated with contracting a venereal disease in the first place.

Counterfeit actions carried out "in the name of God" are just that—counterfeit. Just because someone "claims" that certain actions are sanctioned by God does not mean necessarily that they are. What is needed here is a "fruit inspector" who can compare the counterfeit to the original and thereby separate fact from fiction. J.M. Mathews stated it well: "We ask that the consequences which can be proved to flow from Christianity as the legitimate fruit of the system should be distinguished from those which have no true alliance with her teachings or her influences" (1857, pp. 73-78).

Fourth, speaking of consistency (the topic I used to introduce this section), we need to realize that it is not just the **believer** who should be held to such a standard. The **unbeliever** needs to comply as well. The colloquialism, "The sauce that's good for the goose also is good for the gander," applies here. As Bales observed:

> Atheism and other systems of unbelief, in applying the fruit test to Christianity, are inviting the application of this test to their systems of faith and practice. Atheistic systems undermine the dignity of man by reducing him to an evolved animal; they destroy morality by denying the reality of freedom and the moral law. Any system of strict determinism and moral relativism undermines human dignity and the value of man. When men live by such systems of unbelief, the fruits are destructive. And these destructive fruits are rightly charged to any system which makes man but matter in motion, destroys the moral law, and eliminates the reality of duty. What atheistic materialism does when it rules the lives of men has been demonstrated in our times.... Perhaps this explains why, so far as the author knows, in our country believers in God do not hypocritically put on the cloak of atheism and parade as atheists (1976, pp. 47-48,49).

Bales has made a good point. When you examine the **legitimate** teachings and fruits of a particular system, ask yourself: "Which one has more to commend itself—belief in God, or unbelief?" When Dr. Bales stated that "when men live by such systems of unbelief, the fruits are destructive," he was not speaking out of turn. No less of an authority on atheism than Oxford professor Richard Dawkins conceded as much. In his book, *The Selfish Gene*, Dr. Dawkins discussed at great length the gene's role in the naturalistic process of "survival of the fittest" and admitted that, according to the evolutionary paradigm, genes are "selfish" because they will do whatever it takes to ensure that the individual in which they are stored produces additional copies of the genes. In commenting on the effects of such a concept on society as a whole, he then lamented: "My own feeling is that a human society based simply on the gene's law of universal ruthlessness would be a very nasty society in which to live" (1989b, p. 3).

When men act consistently, when men act congruously, and when men act correctly—in keeping with the cardinal doctrines of their respective world views—which system has more to recommend itself, belief or unbelief? To ask is to answer, is it not? One system—belief—teaches that we should esteem others better than ourselves, love our neighbors, and be self-sacrificing even unto death. The other—unbelief—teaches a "survival of the fittest" concept that makes nature "red in tooth and claw" so that the strong subjugates the weak, might makes right, and "selfish genes" ensure that it is "every man for himself." Truth be told, whom would you rather have for **your** neighbor—the believer, or the unbeliever?

Unbelief

When you see the above section heading of "Unbelief" listed as a **cause** of unbelief, you might think that surely I have erred. How, pray tell, could **unbelief** be a cause of **unbelief**? Please allow me to explain.

It is my contention that unbelief engenders **more** unbelief. In his book, *Therefore Stand*, Wilbur M. Smith compared unchecked unbelief to

> ...a contagious disease. Unless it is restrained it grows in intensity, and will infect an increasingly large number of people. It is difficult to determine whether this is an age of unbelief because so many men do not believe, or many men do not believe because it is an age of unbelief. I suppose that some would say you cannot have an age of unbelief unless it is caused by the unbelief of men. Well, I am not so sure. There are certain intellectual and moral characteristics that mark each age of human history, and it would seem that the outstanding mark of our particular age is Unbelief (1974, p. 173).

Dr. Smith made these comments in the original printing of his book in 1945. If he was correct in his assessment that **his** was an "age of unbelief" (and the documentation he provided incontrovertibly proved his point), then what may be said about **our** age? Smith wrote at a time when America had just emerged from the shadows and ravages of World War II. It was a time in our nation's history when people had sacrificed—first, their finances at home and, second, their sons and daughters on foreign battle fields —to bring an end to tyranny. It also was a time when people actually realized that they **needed** God.

Compare that set of circumstances to those of today. The economy is booming. America has not been involved in a war in over thirty years. Unemployment is at an all-time low. Simply put, people do not feel the "need" for God that they did in post-war America. And there are other factors to be considered. As Smith explained:

> Great thinkers, leaders of thought, men of achievement, men with great gifts of expression, inevitably must influence vast multitudes of people who look up to them as their leaders, as their guide, and when the outstanding men of the great segments of thought in our generation are atheistic, and antagonistic to the Christian Faith, what can one expect the younger generation to be, willingly following in their steps? (1974, p. 174).

We are living in an age where some of the most visible, most respected, and most prolific intellectuals on the world stage are outspoken proponents of unbelief. We view the late Carl Sagan's lavish television extravaganza, *Cosmos*, and are informed that evolution is a "scientific fact" from which no reasonable person dissents. Our children go to their school libraries to select a book for a required reading assignment and are able to choose from over 500 volumes authored by the late evolutionist and humanist, Isaac Asimov, whose vitriolic diatribes against God were his stock-in-trade.

Those same children then go off to college and receive class handouts that are reprints from *Natural History* magazine of the monthly column, "This View of Life," authored by Harvard's renowned Marxist and evolutionist, Stephen Jay Gould. The editors of *National Geographic* send their full-color, slick-paper, professionally produced, eye-catching magazine into our homes each and every month so that we, our children, and our grandchildren can read articles by such world-famous evolutionists as Donald C. Johanson (discoverer of our alleged hominid ancestor, "Lucy") or the late Louis and Mary Leakey (both of whom spent their entire professional careers on the African continent searching for the ever-elusive "missing link" between humans and ape-like ancestors).

Our children sit at the feet of evolutionary professors who strive daily to convince them that they have evolved from some sort of primordial slime on the primeval Earth. They view television shows (produced by amoral unbelievers who have become Hollywood's financial darlings) intended to help rid them of their archaic "Bible-belt mentality." They are required to read and digest articles by atheistic wordsmiths whose purpose it is to convince them that God is no more real than the Man in the Moon or the Easter Bunny. They digest books by prolific, infidelic authors who revel in every facet of human immorality—and who beckon them to do likewise.

Then one day our precious 19- or 20-year-old son or daughter unexpectedly announces, "Mom, Dad, I don't think I believe in God any more." And we stand in shocked amazement—wondering how in the world this could have happened. This is the point I am trying to make when I say that unbelief causes unbelief.

4
CONCLUSION

Every person familiar with the Bible is aware of one of its central themes—the evil results of unbelief. Throughout the Bible, Heaven's warning was that belief (and its accompanying faithfulness) would bring spiritual life and God's blessings, while unbelief (and its accompanying unfaithfulness) would bring God's wrath and spiritual death. The prophet Ezekiel spoke of the man who "turneth away from righteousness and comitteth iniquity, and dieth therein" as being one who "in his iniquity...shall die" (18:26). The apostle Paul observed that the Old Testament was "schoolmaster" (Galatians 3:24) and as such had been penned "for our learning" (Romans 15:4). It should come as no surprise, then, to see Paul catalog in 1 Corinthians 10 a number of instances of apostasy—as a warning to those who might be thinking about following in the footsteps of their unbelieving predecessors.

All too often man's "wisdom" has replaced God's (see 1 Corinthians 1:18-25), causing many to lose their way in what has become one of the most horrible, and yet one of the most common, tragedies of our day. The price humans have paid for being intellectually learned but spiritually ignorant—the loss of their own souls —has been far higher than we ever could have imagined.

In the New Testament book of Mark, there is an intriguing comment about the Lord. The text states simply: "And he could there do no mighty work,...and he marvelled because of their unbelief" (6:5-6). What is the meaning of this statement?

Certainly, it cannot mean that Jesus was **incapable** of performing miracles on this particular occasion. As a member of the Godhead, He was all-powerful (cf. Genesis 17:1, 1 Timothy 6:16), and could not be restrained (cf. Job 42:2). Thus, He could do anything not contradictory to His nature (Habakkuk 1:13; Hebrews 6:18; James 1:13) Performing a miracle certainly was not contradictory to that nature. In fact, on numerous other occasions He had cured those who were blind (Matthew 9:27ff.), deaf and dumb (Mark 7:31ff.), leprous (Luke 17:11ff.), or had crippled limbs (Matthew 9:2; 12:10). He even raised the dead (Luke 7:11ff.). Why, then, does the text specifically record that "he could do there no mighty work"?

When Matthew discussed this event in his Gospel, he wrote: "And he **did not** many mighty works there **because of their unbelief**" (13:58, emp. added). Why, then, did Mark say that the Lord **could not** do mighty works? The Greek employed in Mark's expression is *ouk edunato*. Wayne Jackson has pointed out:

> These words are idiomatically used in the New Testament occasionally to denote what one **deliberately purposed not to do**. Perhaps some examples will be helpful. In one of the Lord's parables, he has a man, who is rejecting the invitation to a great supper, say, "I have married a wife, and therefore I cannot [*ou dunami*] come" (Luke 14:20). It was not that the man was literally unable to attend; rather, for other reasons he **chose not to do so**. Again, John writes: "Whosoever is begotten of God doeth no sin, because his [God's] seed abideth in him: and he cannot [*ou dunatai*] sin, because he is begotten of God" (I Jn. 3:9). This passage teaches that the child of God, because of the seed [the Word of God—Luke 8:11] that abides in him, **chooses** to refrain from practicing a life of habitual sin. So, similarly, the Lord determined not to perform many mighty works in his own country because of the quality of unbelief that was characteristic of them.

This latter observation needs a little amplification. In both Matthew 13:58 and Mark 6:6, the term "unbelief" is preceded by the definite article (*ten*), literally, therefore, "the unbelief of them." Now the Greek article is sort of like an index finger, it points to, draws attention to, an object. Here, it calls attention to the fact that the unbelief of these people was so strong, so downright rebellious, that Jesus would not perform many miracles in their presence in an attempt to coerce them into accepting him (1981, 1:13, emp. and brackets in orig.).

These people had heard the testimony of the many "mighty works" Christ had done throughout the region, and even had witnessed some of His miracles themselves. [The text in Mark indicates that while He did not perform "many" miracles among them, He did heal some of their illnesses (Mark 6:5).] They had the miracle-working Son of God in their midst, and yet their attitude was one of such staunch stubbornness that—in spite of the evidence before them—they steadfastly refused to believe. Today, unbelief often is seen as a "badge of courage" to be displayed openly and worn proudly. Modern spiritual descendants of those first-century unbelievers exhibit what the Hebrew writer termed "an evil heart of unbelief" that has driven them "away from the living God" (Hebrews 10:12).

The Lord was happy to help those of His day whose unbelief resulted from a genuine ignorance of God's teachings. In Mark 9:20-24, the story is told of a father who brought his son to Christ with the request that the Son of God remove the demon that had possessed the youngster from the time he was a small child. The pleading-but-not-quite-able-to-believe father implored the Lord with these words: "If thou canst do anything, have compassion on us, and help us" (9:22). Christ's response to the man's doubt was, "If thou canst! All things are possible to him that believeth" (9:23). Then, "straightway the father of the child cried out, and said, 'I believe; help thou mine unbelief'" (9:24). And the Lord did just that!

The Lord also is happy to help those today who live in honest unbelief, and has provided ample evidence that they might believe. Speaking through the apostle John, God addressed those who, having seen and accepted that evidence, spent a lifetime building their faith upon it. "I am the Alpha and the Omega, the beginning and the end. I will give unto him that is athirst of the fountain of the water of life freely. He that overcometh shall inherit these things; and I will be his God, and he shall be my son" (Revelation 21:6-7).

But what of those who resolutely reject God's message? Their fate, too, was discussed by John: "But for the fearful, and **unbelieving**, and abominable, and murderers, and fornicators, and sorcerers, and idolaters, and all liars, their part shall be in the lake that burneth with fire and brimstone; which is the second death" (Revelation 21:8). Paul, writing to the first-century Christians in Rome, said:

> For the wrath of God is revealed from heaven against all ungodliness and unrighteousness of men, who hinder the truth in unrighteousness; because that which is known of God is manifest in them; for God manifested it unto them. For the invisible things of him since the creation of the world are clearly seen, being perceived through the things that are made, even his everlasting power and divinity; that they may be without excuse: because that, knowing God, they glorified him not as God, neither gave thanks; but became vain in their reasonings, and their senseless heart was darkened. Professing themselves to be wise, they became fools (Romans 1:18-22).

Surely, the words of poet John Greenleaf Whittier are appropriate here: "For all sad words of tongue or pen, the saddest are these: 'It might have been'."

REFERENCES

Abelson, Phillip (1964), "Bigotry in Science," *Science*, vol. 144, April 24.

Arndt, William (1955), Does the Bible Contradict Itself? (St. Louis, MO: Concordia).

Altizer, Thomas J.J. (1961), *Oriental Mysticism and Biblical Eschatology* (Philadelphia, PA: Westminister).

Altizer, Thomas J.J. (1966), *The Gospel of Christian Atheism* (Philadelphia, PA: Westminister).

Asimov, Isaac (1982), "Interview with Isaac Asimov on Science and the Bible," Paul Kurtz, interviewer, *Free Inquiry*, Spring, pp. 6-10. [See also: Hallman, Steve (1991), "Christianity and Humanism: A Study in Contrasts," *AFA Journal*, March, p. 11.]

Ayer, A.J. (1966), "What I Believe," ed. George Unwin, *What I Believe* (London: Allen and Unwin).

Bales, James D. (1967), *The God-Killer?* (Tulsa, OK: Christian Crusade).

Bales, James D. (1976), *How Can Ye Believe?* (Shreveport, LA: Lambert).

Bales, James D. and Robert T. Clark (1966), *Why Scientists Accept Evolution* (Grand Rapids, MI: Baker).

Bertram, George (1971), *"moros," Theological Dictionary of the New Testament*, ed. Gerhard Kittel and Gerhard Friedrich (Grand Rapids, MI: Eerdmans).

Blinderman, Charles S. (1957), "Thomas Henry Huxley," *Scientific Monthly*, April.

Blumenfeld, Samuel L. (1984), *NEA: Trojan Horse in American Education* (Boise, ID: Paradigm).

Brown, Colin (1984), *Miracles and the Critical Mind* (Grand Rapids, MI: Eerdmans).

Christlieb, Theodore (1878), *Modern Doubt and Christian Belief* (New York: Scribner's).

Clark, David K. and Norman L. Geisler (1990), *Apologetics in the New Age: A Critique of Pantheism* (Grand Rapids, MI: Baker).

Clark, Gordon H. (1957), *Thales to Dewey—A History of Philosophy* (Grand Rapids, MI: Baker, 1980 reprint).

Clark, Robert E.D. (1945), *Scientific Rationalism and Christian Faith* (London: Inter-Varsity Fellowship).

Clark, Robert E.D. (1948), *Darwin: Before and After* (London: Paternoster Press).

Coats, Wayne (1989), *The Providence of God*, ed. Thomas B. Warren and Garland Elkins (Southaven, MS: Southaven Church of Christ).

Corduan, Winfried (1993), *Reasonable Faith* (Nashville, TN: Broadman and Holman).

Darwin, Francis (1898), *Life and Letters of Charles Darwin* (New York: D. Appleton).

Davis, Robert Gorham (1997), "Letter to the Editor," *New York Times*, July 5.

Dawkins, Richard, (1989a), "Book Review" (of Donald Johanson & Maitland Edey's *Blueprint*), *The New York Times*, section 7, p. 34, April 9.

Dawkins, Richard (1989b), *The Selfish Gene* (Oxford: Oxford University Press), second edition.

Desmond, Adrian (1997), *Huxley* (Reading, MA: Addison-Wesley).

Desmond, Adrian and James Moore (1991), *Darwin* (New York: Warner).

Dickson, Roger (1979), "The Hermit-God Theology," *Gospel Advocate*, 121[8]:118-119, February 22.

Durant, Will (1961), *The Story of Philosophy* (New York: Simon & Schuster).

Durant, Will (1980), "We Are in the Last Stage of a Pagan Period," *Chicago Tribute Syndicate*, April.

Edwards, Jonathan (1879), *The Works of President Edwards* (New York: Robert Carter and Brothers).

Encyclopaedia Britannica (1997a), s.v. "Agnosticism," (London: Encyclopaedia Britannica, Inc.), 1:151.

Encyclopaedia Britannica (1997b), s.v. "Religious and Spiritual Belief, Systems of," (London: Encyclopaedia Britannica, Inc.), 26:530-577.

Erickson, Millard J. (1992), *Does It Matter What I Believe?* (Grand Rapids, MI: Baker).

Farmer, Herbert H. (1942), *Towards Belief In God* (London: Student Christian Movement Press).

Ferguson, Wallace K. and Geoffrey Bruun (1937), *A Survey of European Civilization: 1500-Present* (Boston: Houghton Mifflin).

Gardner, Martin (1988), *The New Age: Notes of a Fringe Watcher* (Buffalo, NY: Prometheus).

Geisler, Norman L. (1976), *Christian Apologetics* (Grand Rapids, MI: Baker).

Geisler, Norman L. (1997), *Creating God in the Image of Man* (Wheaton, IL: Bethany House).

Geisler, Norman L. and Ronald M. Brooks (1990), *When Skeptics Ask* (Wheaton, IL: Victor Books).

Gould, Stephen Jay (1987), "Darwinism Defined: The Difference Between Fact and Theory," *Discover*, 8[1]:64-65,68-70, January.

Gould, Stephen Jay (1999a), *Rocks of Ages: Science and Religion in the Fullness of Life* (New York: Random House).

Gould, Stephen Jay (1999b), "Dorothy, It's Really Oz," *Time*, 154[8]:59, August 23.

Gould, Stephen Jay and Niles Eldredge (1977), "Punctuated Equilibria: The Tempo and Mode of Evolution Reconsidered," *Paleobiology*, Spring.

Greene, John C. (1963), *Darwin and the Modern World View* (New York: New American Library).

Gruenler, Royce G. (1983), *The Inexhaustible God* (Grand Rapids, MI: Baker).

Hall, Marshall and Sandra Hall (1974), *The Truth: God or Evolution?* (Grand Rapids, MI: Baker).

Harrison, Everett F. (1966), *Baker's Dictionary of Theology* (Grand Rapids, MI: Baker).

Hayes, Judith (1996), *In God We Trust: But Which One?* (Madison, WI: Freedom From Religion Foundation).

Hoover, Arlie J. (1976), *Ideas and Their Consequences* (Abilene, TX: Biblical Research Press).

Hoover, Arlie J. (1981), "Starving the Spirit," *Firm Foundation*, 98[4]:6, January.

Hoyle, Fred and Chandra Wickramasinghe (1981), *Evolution from Space* (London: J.M. Dent).

Huff, Darrell (1959), *How to Take a Chance* (New York: W.W. Norton).

Humanist Manifestos I & II (1973), (Buffalo, NY: Prometheus).

Hurst, Jr., William R. (1971), "Editor's Report," *The [Los Angeles] Herald-Examiner*, section A, p. 4, November 14.

Huxley, Aldous (1966), "Confessions of a Professed Atheist," *Report: Perspective on the News*, 3:19, June.

Huxley, Julian (1960), "At Random: A Television Interview," *Issues in Evolution* (Volume 3 of *Evolution After Darwin*), ed. Sol Tax (Chicago, IL: University of Chicago), pp. 41-65.

Huxley, Julian (1964), *Essays of a Humanist* (New York: Harper & Row).

Huxley, Leonard (1900), *Life and Letters of Thomas Huxley* (New York: Appleton).

Huxley, Thomas Henry (1894), *Collected Essays* (New York: Greenwood Press, 1968 reprint). [Quotation is from volume five of a nine-volume set published 1894-1908.]

Huxley, Thomas Henry (1896), *Darwiniana* (New York: Appleton).

Jackson, Wayne (1981), "'And He Could Do There No Mighty Work'," *Reason and Revelation*, 1:13, April.

Jackson, Wayne (1988), "The Earth: A Planet Plagued with Evil," *Reason and Revelation*, 8:49-52, December.

Jevons, W. Stanley (1928), *Elementary Lessons in Logic* (London: Macmillan).

Johnson, B.C. (1983), *The Atheist Debater's Handbook* (Buffalo, NY: Prometheus).

Keil, C.F. and F. Delitzsch (1981 reprint), *Commentary on the Old Testament* (Grand Rapids, MI: Eerdmans).

Kelcy, Raymond C. (1968), *The Living Word Commentary: The Letters of Paul to the Thessalonians* (Austin, TX: Sweet).

Kennedy, D. James (1997), *Skeptics Answered* (Sisters, OR: Multnomah).

Key, Bobby (1982), "Sin Is a Reproach to Any People," *Four State Gospel News*, 21[12]:2.

Koster, John (1989), *The Atheist Syndrome* (Brentwood, TN: Wolgemuth & Hyatt).

Kreeft, Peter and Ronald K. Tacelli (1994), *Handbook of Christian Apologetics* (Downers Grove, IL: InterVarsity Press).

Kung, Hans (1980), *Does God Exist?* (New York: Doubleday).

Kurtz, Paul (1973), "Scientific Humanism," *The Humanist Alternative*, ed. Paul Kurtz, (Buffalo, NY: Prometheus).

Lamont, Corliss (1949), *Humanism as a Philosophy* (New York: Philosophical Library).

Leakey, Richard and Roger Lewin (1977), *Origins*, New York: E.P. Dutton).

Lewontin, Richard (1997), "Billions and Billions of Demons," *The New York Review*, January 9.

Liebman, Joshua (1946), *Peace of Mind* (New York: Simon & Schuster).

Lippmann, Walter (1929), *A Preface to Morals* (New York: Macmillan).

Lockerbie, D. Bruce (1998), *Dismissing God* (Grand Rapids, MI: Baker).

MacLaine, Shirley (1983), *Out on a Limb* (New York: Bantam).

MacLaine, Shirley (1989), *Going Within* (New York: Bantam).

MacLaine, Shirley (1991), *Dancing in the Light* (New York: Bantam).

Major, Trevor J. (1998), "The Problem of Suffering," *Reason and Revelation*, 18:49-55, July.

Mathews, J.M. (1857), *The Bible and Men of Learning* (New York: Daniel Fanshaw).

McClintock, John and James Strong (1879), *Cyclopedia of Biblical, Theological, and Ecclesiastical Literature* (Grand Rapids, MI: Baker, 1970 reprint).

McGrath, Alister E. (1993), *Intellectuals Don't Need God* (Grand Rapids, MI: Zondervan).

Medawar, Peter (1968), "On 'The Effecting of All Things Possible'," *The Listener*, October 2.

Montgomery Advertiser (1999), "Atheists Move Headquarters," April 3, Section D, p. 3.

Morris, Henry M. (1963), *Twilight of Evolution* (Grand Rapids, MI: Baker).

Morris, Henry M. (1971), *The Bible Has the Answer* (Nutley, NJ: Craig Press).

Morris, Henry M. (1989), *The Long War Against God* (Grand Rapids, MI: Baker).

O'Hair, Madalyn Murray (1983), "Introduction," *Sixty-five Press Interviews with Robert G. Ingersoll* (Austin, TX: American Atheist Press).

Prabhavananda, Swami and Christopher Isherwood (1972), "Appendix II: The Gita War," in *Bhagavad Gita* (Bergerfield, NJ: New American Library).

Raymo, Chet (1998), *Skeptics and True Believers* (New York: Walker).

Rehwinkel, Alfred (1951), *The Flood* (St. Louis, MO: Concordia).

Ricci, Paul (1986), *Fundamentals of Critical Thinking* (Lexington, MA: Ginn Press).

Ruse, Michael and Edward O. Wilson (1985), "Evolution and Ethics," *New Scientist*, vol. 208, October 17.

Sagan, Carl (1980), *Cosmos* (New York: Random House).

Samuel, (1950), *The Impossibility of Agnosticism* [a tract], (Downers Grove, IL: InterVarsity Press).

Sartre, Jean Paul, (1961), "Existentialism and Humanism," *French Philosophers from Descartes to Sartre*, ed. Leonard M. Marsak (New York: Meridian).

Sauer, Erich (1962), *The King of the Earth* (Grand Rapids, MI: Eerdmans).

Sayers, Stanley (1973), *Optimism in an Age of Peril* (Delight, AR: Gospel Light).

Simpson, George Gaylord (1953), *Life of the Past* (New Haven, CT: Yale University Press).

Simpson, George Gaylord (1964), *This View of Life* (New York: Harcourt- Brace).

Sire, James W. (1988), *The Universe Next Door* (Downers Grove, IL: InterVarsity Press).

Smith, David (1910), *Man's Need of God* (London: Hodder and Stoughton).

Smith, F. LaGard (1986), *Out on a Broken Limb* (Eugene, OR: Harvest House).

Smith, George H. (1979), *Atheism: The Case Against God* (Buffalo, NY: Prometheus).

Smith, Huston (1982), "Evolution and Evolutionism," *Christian Century*, July 7-14.

Smith, Nelson M. (1975), "The Case Against Agnosticism," *Firm Foundation*, 92[6]:6,11, February.

Smith, Wilbur M. (1974 reprint), *Therefore Stand* (Grand Rapids, MI: Baker).

Sproul, R.C. (1978), *If There's a God, Why Are There Atheists?* (Wheaton, IL: Tyndale House).

Story, Dan (1997), *Defending Your Faith* (Grand Rapids, MI: Kregel).

Taylor, Ian (1984), *In the Minds of Men* (Toronto, Canada: TFE Publishing).

Templeton, Charles B. (1996), *Farewell to God* (Toronto, Ontario, Canada: McClelland and Stewart).

Thompson, Bert (1990), "Does Human Suffering Disprove the Existence of a Benevolent God?," *Giving a Reason for Our Hope*, ed. Winford Claiborne (Henderson, TN: Freed-Hardeman College), pp. 280-285).

Thompson, Bert (1993), "Do Natural Disasters Negate Divine Benevolence?," *Reason and Revelation*, 13:65-69, September.

Thompson, Bert (1994), "Famous Enemies of Christ," *Reason & Revelation*, 14:1-7, January.

Thompson, Bert (1995a), "The Case for the Existence of God—[Part I]," *Reason and Revelation*, 15:33-38, May.

Thompson, Bert (1995b), "The Case for the Existence of God—[Part II]," *Reason and Revelation*, 15:41-47, June.

Thompson, Bert (1999), "The Many Faces of Unbelief—[Part II]," *Reason & Revelation* 19:25-31, April.

Thompson, Bert and Wayne Jackson (1982), "The Revelation of God in Nature," *Reason and Revelation*, 2:17-24, May.

Thompson, Bert and Wayne Jackson (1996), *The Case for the Existence of God* (Montgomery, AL: Apologetics Press).

Thompson, Bert and Wayne Jackson (1992), *A Study Course in Christian Evidences* (Montgomery, AL: Apologetics Press).

Van Biema, David (1997), "Where's Madalyn?," *Time*, 149[6]:56-60, February 10.

Watkin, Edward I. (1936), *Theism, Agnosticism and Atheism* (London: Unicorn Press).

Watson, James D. (1968), *The Double Helix* (New York: Atheneum).

Weinberg, Steven (1993), *Dreams of a Final Theory* (New York: Vintage Books).

Wilson, Edward O. (1982), "Toward a Humanistic Biology," *The Humanist*, September/October.

Woods, Guy N. (1982), "'And be not Conformed to this World'," *Gospel Advocate*, 124[1]:2, January 7.

Young, Robert M. (1982), "The Darwin Debate," *Marxism Today*, vol. 26. NOTE: In this article, in speaking of Harvard evolutionist Stephen Jay Gould, Young has suggested that Dr. Gould is "avowedly non-Marxist." This, however, is incorrect. Gould has admitted, under oath, that he is a Marxist [see: Morris, Henry M. (1982), *Evolution in Turmoil* (San Diego, CA: Creation-Life Publishers), pp. 102-103].

Zerr, E.M. (1952), *Bible Commentary* (Bowling Green, KY: Guardian of Truth).